BRICK WONDERS

Contents

WELCOME TO BRICK WONDERS

As a LEGO® fan myself, I've attended numerous shows, conventions, and LEGO exhibitions. I think I must have seen almost everything depicted in LEGO—from castles to marinas, and spaceships to dragons. So when the opportunity to write the sequel to *Brick City* arose, it only seemed natural to throw the net as wide as possible—to cover thousands of years of history and every continent on the planet. Then, we really could show the *Brick Wonders* of the world.

The original list, the seven wonders of the ancient world, was believed to have been compiled by the historian Herodotus around 450 B.C. At that time, the list included six of the recognized seven wonders. The Lighthouse of Alexandria was not yet built, so the Ishtar Gate inside Babylon was counted instead. The number seven must have remained significant, as in the Middle Ages the Ishtar Gate was replaced by the Lighthouse of Alexandria to form the group that we know today.

Of course, the seven wonders of the ancient world are just that—from ancient times. More telling, perhaps, is the fact that most were European. Historical records of the Americas, the Far East, and Australasia had yet to reach scholars. So, whereas *Brick Wonders* covers each of these seven ancient wonders, I decided to add in some more modern (and more ancient) wonders as well.

The first part of this book recreates each of the seven ancient wonders in my favorite format: LEGO bricks. Each of the wonders is recreated to show its majesty and scale, and I have included detailed instructions for elements of each wonder that you can build at home. Of course, most of these ancient wonders no longer exist, and some are lost almost entirely to history. So bear with me as I make some educated guesses as to what they might have looked like.

For the next part of *Brick Wonders*, we look elsewhere to the ancient world and to the parts of the world that those ancient scholars were unaware of. We visit South America, China, the Middle East, and medieval London as I choose seven wonders from history. These wonders combine unique geography and human endeavor to create some astounding feats of engineering and design.

Bringing the book right up-to-date, the third part of *Brick Wonders* looks at our modern wonders. Seven

inventions that have changed the world—or even left it. From the Internet to the media, and transportation to medicine, these seven wonders have reshaped the world that we live in and made our modern lifestyles possible. We even leave Earth briefly as the International Space Station flies past.

In the final part of the book, I take a look at seven wonders that have outlived all of the others—my natural wonders of the world. This part takes us to the farthest reaches of our planet. The Great Barrier Reef in Australia teams with life, as does the African Savanna. The final part of the book also takes us to our final continent—Antarctica—as we wonder at the Aurora Australis.

I hope you enjoy *Brick Wonders*—whether you decide to build any of the models, or just admire the images. And remember, if you want to build your own wonders but don't have the bricks I've used, don't worry. Build from your heart and your imagination, and you can't go wrong building your own brick wonder.

– Warren Elsmore

HISTORY OF LEGO®

The story began in 1916 when Ole Kirk Christiansen started a woodworking business in Billund, Denmark. He made wooden toys at first, and by the 1930s had dubbed the company "LEGO" after an abbreviation of the Danish phrase that means "play well." The company moved into plastics in 1947, and in 1949 they began producing plastic interlocking bricks under the name "Automatic Binding Bricks."

The early designs were not quite the bricks we know today, but in 1954 Ole Kirk's son, Godtfred, conceived that with the addition of doors and windows, LEGO bricks (so named in 1953) had almost limitless creative potential. The first town-plan system was released soon after, but LEGO bricks were still not the company's core business. The stud-and-tube interlocking system was developed and patented in 1958, and bricks from this date are still compatible with the ones for sale today—the most important innovation was that when they were snapped together, they remained in place. That was the year Ole Kirk died, and the business passed to Godtfred. In 1960, a warehouse fire destroyed much of the remaining stock of wooden toys, and production of them was discontinued. The company was now comprised of more than 400 employees and poised to enter the United States, Canada, and Italy. Within a few years, it spread to a host of other countries,

including Finland, the Netherlands, Hong Kong, Australia, Morocco, and Japan. The LEGO® invasion had begun.

By 1966 the toys were in 42 countries, and the first LEGO train had been introduced, running on a four-and-a-half-volt motor. This was also the year that the first LEGOLAND Park was opened, in Billund, Denmark, receiving 3,000 visitors on its first day.

Sets have continued to be released on many different themes, from spacecrafts to pirate ships, and many technical elements have been incorporated, such as motors, magnets, and sensors. LEGO Duplo—larger bricks for younger children—were released in 1977, and the following year miniature figurines (minifigs) followed, allowing humanoid shapes to inhabit the LEGO landscapes for the first time.

LEGO has inspired many people to accomplish extraordinary feats over the years, and encouraged so much energetic innovation that few records set for LEGO creations last very long. One which has lasted (so far) is the largest LEGO structure, a statue of the Sitting Bull at LEGOLAND, Denmark, which stands at almost 25 feet tall (7.75 meters) and was made from one and a half million bricks. At the time of writing, the tallest LEGO tower is a staggering 112 feet, eleven inches (32.5 meters), constructed by Red Clay Consolidated School, Wilmington.

I'm also proud to have my own little piece of record history. In 2012 at my LEGO Show, the largest mosaic in the world was constructed—1,549 square feet and three square inches (144 square meters), meaning that I'm the happy owner of a Guinness World Record certificate. Since then, though, the record has already been beaten at least twice. Such is the fervor and dedication of LEGO builders, these records really don't last long.

The Great Wall was built by a series of ancient Chinese emperors, see pages 86–89 for the model.

WHERE TO BUY LEGO®

HOW TO FIND THE BRICKS YOU'LL NEED

Real-world architecture is much more serious than the LEGO sets you find in the shops, so many of the models in this book will use repeating patterns of bricks—or huge numbers of the same piece. This is where your special LEGO-buying skills come in.

The first piece of advice is to pull together all the existing bricks you have. LEGO is such a popular toy, it's almost certain that somewhere in your attic, basement, or parents' house, there are boxes of LEGO parts lying around. Dig through, see if you have the bricks you need or bricks that will do (if you can't find a certain brick, for example a 2x4 brick, try a substitute, such as two 2x2 bricks), and get building. Chances are that you will find most of the bricks you need, and if you can forgive a little color variation, you're all set.

But of course, there are models that just have to be built in the right color and/or the right bricks. The Great Wall on page 86 looks great in tan, and white would probably work well too. But the impact would have been lost if twelve colors were used to make the front. So where does a craftsman source bricks?

If you live in Denmark, the United States, Canada, the United Kingdom, Germany, France, Malaysia, Belgium, or Austria, you may have a local LEGO brand store or LEGOLAND theme park. These stores have special "Pick a Brick" areas: a wall of containers holding all different parts. Need some lime green 2x4 bricks? Here you can buy them by the bucket-load. If that sounds similar to choosing candy at the movies, that's because it is. Pick a Brick walls are a great resource, and as bricks are typically sold by volume or weight, this can work out to be a highly cost-effective way to buy bricks.

If you're not near a LEGO store or LEGOLAND park, don't despair; you can still access Pick a Brick online, which is available though LEGO's website at *www.lego.com* and delivers to a wide range of countries. The online shop charges per part, so you should determine precisely what you need before placing an order.

The vast majority of the models with instructions in this book are designed so you can build them from parts available either online or in a LEGO store. However, sometimes a specific part is needed to make a model work, and although they were all made by LEGO, not every part has remained in production over its 50-year history. The answer is to be found on *www.bricklink.com*, the brainchild of an enterprising young LEGO enthusiast, Dan Jezek (who is sadly no longer with us). Here, thousands of traders worldwide list the parts they want to sell so that LEGO fans can source whichever parts they need (you will need a PayPal account to buy from most sellers, and this is encouraged as it has built-in protection). You should also always take note of the seller's location, as a part might be cheap, but shipping prices and import duty can make the purchase much less appealing. You may also want to keep an eye on your wallet—once you get used to the luxury of unlimited LEGO parts available at the press of a button, it can get expensive very quickly.

Building Tips

One thing you might notice as you flip through this book is that the LEGO® models featured don't look like the LEGO models you might see on the shelves of your local toy store. Well, there's a reason for that. The first question I'm asked about a model is usually: "Is that really all LEGO?" The answer is yes. Every model you see here is made from 100 percent LEGO elements. But the way in which these bricks are assembled might significantly vary from what you're used to.

Many of the icons within these pages are built "studs up"—that is, each brick is stacked on top of the one beneath it. Many other models, however, are not built this way. To understand why not, we need to go back to school…

There are two basic types of LEGO elements from which nearly all other elements are derived: bricks and plates. One LEGO brick is equal in height to three LEGO plates. Plates give models more rigidity (for instance, they make great floors), but they also allow you to have three times the color variation or detail in the same space as a simple brick. Smaller elements mean more accurate designs, so many of the models in this book will use plates instead of bricks wherever possible. For instance, as below a colored stripe can be introduced by using three plates of contrasting colors rather than a single brick.

Yet making models out of plates will only take us so far. Skyscrapers and flat-sided vehicles adapt well, but what about curved surfaces, thin extrusions, and structural steelwork? How do we model those in LEGO? Thankfully there are many other bricks which can help us out—thousands of types of elements, dating back over fifty years. Roofs can be made out of sloped bricks, and steel columns can be represented by LEGO Technic elements—and you will see many more examples in our instruction illustrations. Choosing the right elements can help create a model in a surprisingly small number of parts.

There is another important technique that LEGO fans use to put bricks together, which is nicknamed "SNOT." This stands for "Studs Not On Top"— turning bricks or plates sideways enables countless other possibilities.

SNOT relies on another simple principle of LEGO geometry. Whereas a LEGO brick is three times the height of a LEGO plate, it is also two and a half times as wide as that plate is high. Or, two bricks equal five plates, as in the image below.

Using plates and SNOT, the accuracy of our modeling can be increased threefold, in all directions. And this brings even more interesting possibilities. Perhaps a model needs a circle not available from LEGO® as an existing element? Whereas it would be possible to use plates to model this curve—and they would work well for part of the circle—this method is not so useful as the curve becomes steeper. But turn half the plates sideways and suddenly our model is far more accurate.

To hold these sideways elements in place, we need some special pieces which can hold elements on one side, two sides, or even all four sides of a brick, and luckily a number of these exist. In the end, a combination of bricks and plates, and the use of all the available slopes, hinges, curves, and of course SNOT, enables us to make the models in this book possible.

Modeling a curve without SNOT

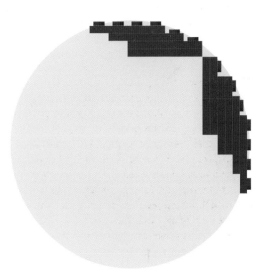

Modeling a curve using SNOT

CAD Modeling

No matter how many LEGO® bricks you might own, you'll certainly never have enough. How do you build your favorite model without having all of the rights bricks at hand? When designing the models for *Brick Wonders*, I've use LEGO CAD software.

CAD (Computer Aided Design) software lets you play with virtual LEGO bricks to create an amazing model. With an unlimited number of bricks at your disposal, in any color you like, there's nothing to stop you from creating the ultimate LEGO model. There are two main types of LEGO CAD systems available, and both are free.

LEGO Digital Designer (*ldd.lego.com*) is available for free download from LEGO and available for either Mac or PC. Once you have installed the software, it will download a full list of all the (currently) available LEGO bricks for you to build with. Expect this to take some time as there are a lot of bricks to choose between.

The newer versions of LEGO Digital Designer now include a standard or "Extended Mode." While "standard" mode will only allow you to use bricks in

colors that exist, "Extended Mode" doesn't have such a restriction—letting you build your models from a huge range of bricks.

One of the real benefits of LDD is that it's designed to help you build a creation that will work in the real world—so bricks will be automatically connected for you as you place them. Once finished, LDD can even create on-line instructions automatically so you can build the model in the real world. Just switch the model into "Building Guide Mode" and follow the steps.

The LDraw system (*www.ldraw.org*) is the second type of LEGO CAD system available. LDraw predates LDD, and rather than being written by the LEGO Group, the LDraw system was created and is maintained by the LEGO community themselves. Fans like you and me.

So if LEGO produces free design software, why use anything else? Well, for me LDraw has a few significant advantages. Firstly, almost any part—ever made—is available in the LDraw system. That's a much larger list than what's available in LDD, and sometimes an older

Various screen shots showing LEGO CAD designs used in this book.

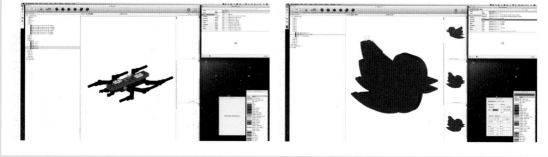

part works perfectly to recreate a feature in a certain model. Every single part has been painstakingly drawn based on the physical components.

Secondly, editing software using the LDraw system is far more flexible than LEGO® Digital Designer. For instance, the tool I use—Bricksmith—will let you create models that wouldn't really work in the real world. When designing a model, I sometimes just use a 1x1 brick for everything—to layout the overall shape. Of course, if I tried to do that in real life, the model would just fall apart. Modeling on the computer though, that's not something I need to worry about—it's much faster when you don't have to worry about how a model might actually stay together.

When building a larger creation, it's also handy to be able to do things that wouldn't work in real life while I fine tune a model. The ability to place 2 bricks in the same physical space means that I can slide bricks along without worrying about the studs. It's also a very easy task to replace two 1x4 bricks with a 1x8 brick—without being concerned about the bricks above or below it.

There is a down side to all this flexibility, of course. Using the LDraw system, you will have to work out for yourself how to build that model so it will hold together, and then you need to create your own instructions. The benefits outweigh these disadvantages for me though, and it's LDraw that I've used for all the models in this book.

The LDraw system supports a wide range of different tools that you can use to create models and instructions. Although each tool works slightly differently, they do all use the same core library of parts. For this book, I have used the Bricksmith editor on the Mac to create all the models and the LPub tool to create their instructions. I am extremely grateful to all those involved for their hard work in creating this software, and to everyone involved at LDraw.org.

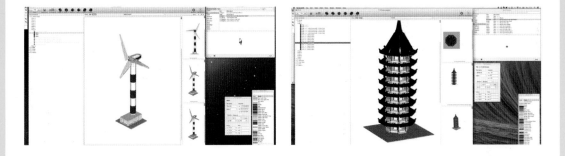

FREESTYLE

BUILD LEGO® FREESTYLE, WITHOUT A SET OF INSTRUCTIONS

Free building is a little like free climbing—there's no safety net. The majority of the models in this book are not free builds because they have to be as precise as possible, and require a lot of work, so it is best to use instructions. But the truth is, freestyle is how most people build and have fun with LEGO, because it allows you to really use your imagination and make good use of your hidden creative talent. It's easy to come up with an idea for a model based on a random assortment of bricks—try it for yourself.

Anything can be built freestyle. A child might build a spaceship out of whichever parts are available and believe it is one. But as we get older, however, we get fixed ideas about what a spaceship looks like and might decide in advance whether it has

rockets, blasters, and a sleek, domed cockpit. The trick to enjoying free building is to try and forget that strict, specific approach and the need for exact accuracy, and to reinvent your creations with that childlike imagination.

Here's a tip for a good way to encourage yourself to free build. At your next adult dinner party, go to your local toy store and find some small sets, getting one for every guest. Something from the creator range is good—they tend to have lots of pieces and a low price point. Now, your challenge is to free build from that set only. Perhaps choose a spaceship (or robot, car, or house) as a theme, and sit back. You'll be amazed what you and your guests can come up with—even if childhood was technically decades ago.

Use your imagination to turn a pile of assorted bricks into a wonderful freestyle model.

INSTRUCTIONS

One question that I'm often asked is if all my models have instructions. Whereas many of the models in *Brick Wonders* do contain instructions, you'll notice that a good number do not. To understand why I don't produce instructions for every model, it will probably help to understand the process behind this.

To create instructions for the models in *Brick Wonders*, I first build the model itself in the LDraw CAD system. Using LDraw means that I can create accurate instructions very similar to those you might find in an official LEGO® set. The images are produced electronically to have a consistent look and feel, and the colors are easy to distinguish.

However, there are some models that are very difficult to model in CAD software. If a model has a curved surface or perhaps hinges, then when building the model with real bricks, it's very easy to see if the bricks will connect. They will either snap together or not. However, as the CAD software allows bricks to overlap each other, it's much harder to see if the bricks will connect or not. The Lighthouse at Alexandria on page 80, for instance, would be very hard to model in CAD as it contains many hinged surfaces.

Certain models also present problems of scale. Whereas, for instance, it would be possible to model the container ship from the Panama Canal on page 146 in CAD, the resulting set of instructions would be enormous. With some models using tens of thousands of bricks, the instructions for a model of this scale would fill this entire book. Leaving out instructions for these models gives us space to include more exciting models for you to build.

Once I've created a CAD model of the LEGO model, then it's time to start thinking about how the model should be built. The CAD software I use doesn't automatically create each step of the instructions, so I need to decide how many stages a model should have and which bricks need to be added at what stage. This step of the process can actually be quite difficult—I don't want to make the instructions too hard to follow, but they shouldn't be too long either. In many of the models I've designed, certain parts are held in strange ways or perhaps not connected to other parts until much later. This introduces more complexity as well.

Finally, once I've decided on the steps for the instructions, I use the LPub program to render these steps into individual images for you to follow. LPub also automatically creates the list of parts that you need for each step. Each set of instructions needs some small changes to make sure that it is easily readable, then it's over to you.

If the model that you want to build doesn't have instructions, though, don't worry. There's no "right" or "wrong" way to build a LEGO model. As long as you have a model that you are proud of, that's all that matters. Remember, LEGO bricks are a toy, so you should always have fun building.

Naming Bricks

What do you call this element?

I'd refer to it as a 2x4 brick, but perhaps it's a 4x2 brick? Or an "eight-er" or even a "Rory?" Did you know that all LEGO® elements have official names? If you're buying parts to build some of the models from *Brick Wonders*, it will probably help to know what these names are.

There are two main naming schemes for LEGO elements. The first, of course, is from The LEGO Group, which obviously has a name for each brick it produces.

The second naming scheme is used by the adult fans of LEGO within LDraw and BrickLink.

The LEGO naming scheme is fairly straightforward—with a few exceptions. The basic unit is of course a brick—like this 1x1 brick on the left.

From there, the naming references the short side first. So these are 1x1, 1x2, 1x3, and 1x4 bricks:

Of course, you might call the longer brick a "four-er." But then, how would you distinguish between these bricks? They all have four studs.

This is why most LEGO fans will use the same naming, so it's easier to ask our friends if they have any 2x2 round bricks or 1x4 bricks. A common naming convention means that we're both looking for the same part. Of course, once your bricks are organized, then it's time to move onto "plates," "tiles," and "slopes." The same naming structure applies, and now you have the four basic types of elements that LEGO produces.

Of course, there are many, many other types of element produced, many of which are highly specialized and look nothing like a brick. So in general, I use the term "elements" to refer to LEGO parts, whatever the shape, especially when special bricks are involved. This, for instance, is a 1x1 Brick with One Knob.

NAMING BRICKS

As The LEGO® Group is a Danish company, the word "knob" is the English translation of a Danish word. This is also where the fan naming tends to diverge from LEGO's own names—partly because of the influence of American fans and the English language on the Internet. In English, at least, the protruding part of the brick is called a "stud" rather than a "knob." Of course, that varies by country as well—the Dutch would call it a "nop" and the Danish, "knop." Matters become even more complicated when you're dealing with arch bricks.

So, which name is "correct?" Well, whereas the LEGO name might be the official name, that's not to say that any other name is wrong. The brick on the left, for instance, is a 1x2 Palisade Brick.

But ask any fan for a Palisade Brick, and they won't know what you are talking about. To fans, this is a 1x2 Log Brick and this is where the problems lie. The chances are that you, like me, will order bricks from LEGO and also from BrickLink, or buy them from other fans. So, sadly, there's no real easy way around it. In some cases, you just need to know both names. Especially with bricks like this one to the right, which is both Brick 2x1x1&⅓ with Curved Top OR Brick W. Arch 1x1x1⅓.

1x4 Arch Brick OR Brick with Bow 1x4 and 1x4 Curved Slope OR… Brick with Bow 1x4

BUILDING FOR STRENGTH

If you're going to construct a *Brick Wonder* of your own, one of the problems that you might encounter would be to make your structure strong enough to last. Perhaps not thousands of years—but at least long enough to show your friends.

While making a model completely solid might seem like a good way of making a strong model, it's a technique that I don't often use, and you might not either. Creating a completely solid model is a very costly technique—both in terms of time and bricks. But there's another problem too. A solid model will be very heavy and has a tendency to split. With no flexibility in the model, it can break easily. So, how to build a strong model?

The first technique in building a strong model is a simple one. Overlap your bricks wherever possible. A stack of 1x2 bricks placed next to each other will have very little strength, but overlap them as real bricks are overlapped and you'll find them much, much stronger.

If you're building a landscape or larger model, you might need to create some internal supports to hold up a roof or floor level. Again, creating these from overlapping bricks will save you time and weight. If you make sure to connect them well at roof level, you'll create a strong and light mesh that will travel well.

One tip that might not seem obvious at first is that you don't need to connect all the studs of a large building together, or at least not in certain ways. While you might think that two large plates pushed on top of each other would create a very strong base, you'll find that as the sizes increase this becomes harder and harder. Try putting two 16x16 plates on top of each other for instance, or perhaps don't. The problem will be that with so many studs connecting to each other, it's unlikely that you'll get them all pushed together properly. The studs in the middle of a plate will bow as the air is trapped.

To create a really strong base, try creating a plate–brick–plate sandwich. A flat layer of plates, followed by overlapping bricks (1x16 bricks are great for this), and then another layer of plates. That will create a strong surface that won't deform.

If your wonder is really large, you'll probably start to wonder about how to move it around, too. Large models are great, but there always comes a time when it has to be moved around. For this, I'd suggest looking to the larger models produced by The LEGO® Group—the modular buildings. These sets build a 3 or even 4 story building that can be easily dissected.

The secret is to build in layers, connecting each layer with either a lip formed of tiles or the new 1x4 plate with 2 studs. These new plates are great for managing where walls might come apart in your model. They have great sticking power to the bricks below them (called "clutch power" in LEGO terms), but less clutch power to the bricks above them. So you can create a point at which it's easy to take a model apart.

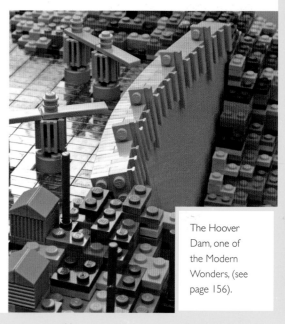

The Hoover Dam, one of the Modern Wonders, (see page 156).

PRACTICE PROJECT

Before we begin our trip through history, it might be worth brushing up on those LEGO® building skills. Although I've tried to make the instructions in this book as clear to follow as possible, some of the building techniques might be new to you if you've not played with LEGO in a while.

So, here's your chance to learn. From the Gutenberg Press model on page 166 in Modern Wonders, I've selected one of the moveable type characters to show you how to build the lettering. Once you've mastered the letter "B," the rest should be easy.

Once you've built the first few layers of bricks, you'll notice the first technique I've used. I wanted to make sure that my letter "B" had curved edges, but the part that I was using (Brick 2×1×1&⅓ with Curved Top, or part 6091 for easier reference) only comes in one variation. There is a curve down, but no corresponding curved up part. To overcome this, I've had to build parts of the letter upside down.

The next difference you might notice in these instructions is that I don't build the whole model as one piece. In this model, as with many official LEGO models, I've built lots of "submodels." In this case, because parts of the model are built upside down, if I were to create instructions layer by layer, you'd find

that the parts would fall apart when building it. So instead I've created submodels which you build first, then attach to the main model. This should (hopefully) make the models easier to build.

There is also another trick that I've used while building this letter that you'll very rarely see official LEGO sets use. There are quite a few parts of this model that are not connected to anything. As parts of the model are upside down, I'm not able to connect them together using studs as I would on a normal model. There are ways to do this, using headlight bricks (part 4070), for instance, as seen on the Twitter logo on page 188. However, in this case, I've gone for a simple solution, creating two parts of the model that interlock together.

So, now that you've built the letter "B," it's time to try the rest of the word "BRICK"—but there aren't any instructions this time. That's part of the fun, though. Although many of the *Brick Wonders* models do have instructions, there are also many that don't. It's up to you and your imagination to create these models and create your own wonders.

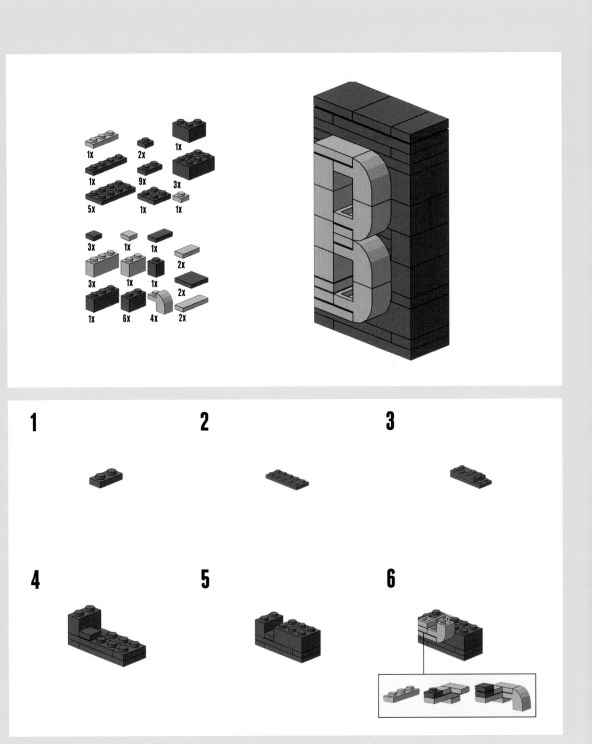

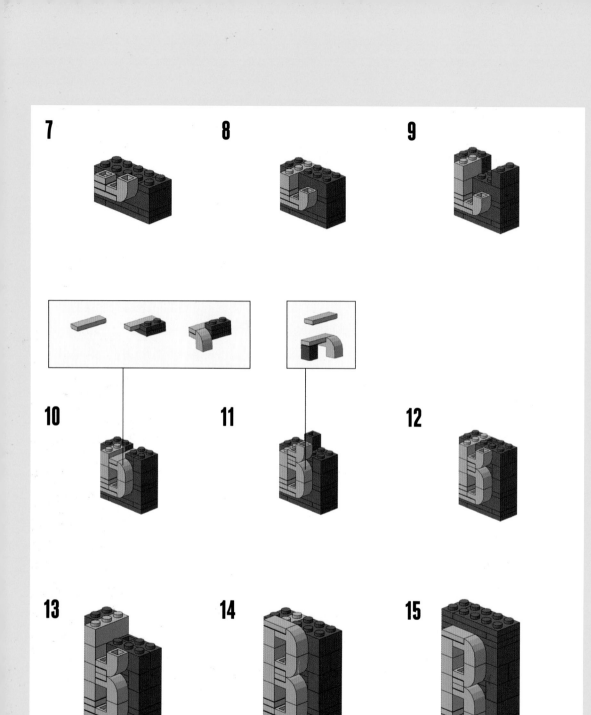

The Gutenberg
Printing Press
on page 166—a
wonder of the
modern world.

MOSAICS

LEGO® mosaics are, in principle, very straightforward. There are a limited number of LEGO colors, but thankfully more than enough to create a good picture. So the difficulties you may encounter will be related to the choice of image and how best to bring that out in LEGO tiles. There are a few tips that we can use to help us along the way.

Choosing your mosaic picture is the first challenge. You may be creating a mosaic of yourself, your favorite cartoon character, or any other image you like. To create a mosaic with maximum impact, try to stay away from images which are particularly complex. The more shades or fine detail an image has, the harder it will be to convert that into a recognizable LEGO mosaic—at least without making it absolutely enormous. So if you can, stick to a simple image with bold colors and features. I'm going to assume from here that you have this image on your computer.

There are many ways of converting your image into a LEGO mosaic. Really, a LEGO mosaic is just a low-resolution version of the image. You can try reducing the definition of the picture on your computer until it starts to become pixelated, as though it's made from LEGO tiles. However, this doesn't always work: you will often find that the image becomes unrecognizable, or that there are too many colors in it. This is where LEGO mosaic software comes in handy.

There are lots of software programs that will let you turn your image into a LEGO mosaic by reducing the colors and size down automatically. I've used Pictobrick (*www.pictobrick.de*) and Photobricks (*www.photobricksapp.com*) for the mosaics in this book. Both are fairly simple to use, and will ask you how large you'd like the mosaic and what method to use to cut down the number of colors. Once finished, you'll get an output of what bricks go where and you just copy the image down in LEGO.

Anything is possible with a LEGO mosaic. World records are toppling all the time, with mosaics regularly being built from more than a million bricks. So think of your favorite image, and if you have the desire to build it, it can be done.

The Aurora Australis mosaic, one of the Natural Wonders on page 198.

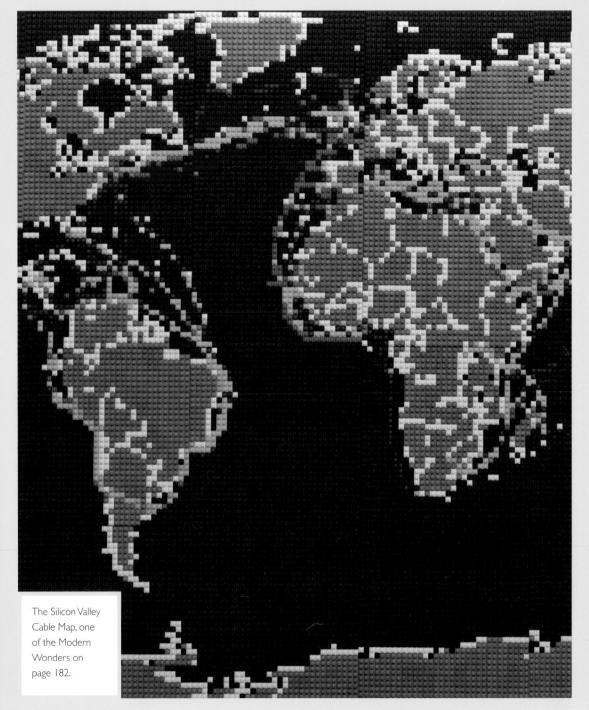

The Silicon Valley Cable Map, one of the Modern Wonders on page 182.

SORTING AND STORING

There is one perennial problem when it comes to LEGO® bricks—sorting them. Unless you have a very small collection, it soon becomes apparent that trying to find the right LEGO element can take more time than actually building the model. So, what to do? What is the best way of sorting your bricks?

If you have a very small collection—perhaps only one or two sets—then the obvious way to sort your LEGO is to not sort it at all. With not many bricks to choose between, storing all the bricks in one box is an appealing thought. Having said that, though, even if you have a large amount of LEGO, there is a benefit to this approach. Although I build in a studio, with huge numbers of bricks available in every color, sometimes my most creative builds come from using only a small number of parts. Or building from a mixed pile of LEGO—taking inspiration from the parts available at hand. Not sorting your LEGO can actually help sometimes.

As your LEGO collection grows, however, most people will choose to sort their LEGO so it's easier to store and build from. There are lots of ways to do this, but the most common methods chosen are either by color or by brick. Sorting by color is often the first way that LEGO fans decide to arrange their bricks. If you want to make a white house, then surely it's easier to build from a box of white bricks?

Sorting by color has one distinct disadvantage, though—black. Sorting through a box of black bricks is very difficult unless you have very bright lights. Black parts all seem to combine together so that you can never find the part you're looking for. As your collection grows, you'll also start to find that sorting by color becomes unmanageable. When you have one very large box of blue, how can you find that one blue 1x2 Brick with Studs on Both Sides that you need?

Progressing from sorting by color, many fans then sort by type. Each different element has its own drawer or box, so it's easy to find a part. As your collection grows, you realize that perhaps every part having a drawer isn't so practical—you would need tens of thousands of drawers. So, elements are grouped together—all the LEGO Technic elements are stored together, perhaps, or all the tiles. Sorting by part works well for most medium-sized collections.

When you progress into "Master Builder" territory, or build professionally for a living like I do, then you need an approach that scales well. My studio contains many hundreds of thousands of bricks—almost certainly millions although I've never counted. Professional builders mainly choose to sort by both part AND color. This means that it's easy to find one exact piece, but we can also quickly get hold of, for instance, all the gray bricks.

Sort your bricks by color or type in clearly labeled drawers.

Each builder will have their own system that works for them the best. In fact, I actually have two systems running concurrently in my studio.

When I'm planning a build, what's most important to me is the way that the bricks connect. So inside my office, the walls are surrounded by hundreds of small drawers—the same drawers that are used for storing screws. In these drawers, I keep elements by part, regardless of color. This means that if I want to check how one brick connects to another, I can quickly find the parts and check. Color isn't important to me here, as I'm usually prototyping a design to check if something will work correctly.

However, when I'm building a large model, such as the ones in *Brick Wonders*, it's important that I have the right shape and color of bricks. So this is where my main stores come into play. I store my bricks by part and by color. At the moment, my primary sort is by color, so I have a green section, a blue section, etc. Then within each section, I have a number of drawers, and within each drawer are the parts themselves. To make sure that the parts don't mix together, I store each part/color combination in a resealable bag.

So, if I'm building a small, quick model, I have everything at hand from my chair. If I'm building a large model, I can select the bags of parts that I need—or perhaps even remove entire drawers if I know I'll need, for instance, lots of white bricks.

There's only one real problem with having a well-sorted and stored LEGO collection. You do, of course, have to sort the bricks first!

Larger drawers can be used to sort various bags containing different parts.

ONLINE RESOURCES

LEGO® fans of all ages have a huge and vibrant community, both in person and online. So if you've been inspired by *Brick Wonders*, why not get involved yourself?

LEGO MESSAGE BOARDS

Most peoples' earliest interaction with other LEGO fans online is possibly through the LEGO Message Boards at *community.LEGO.com*. The LEGO Message Boards are the company's official forums run by The LEGO Group. The Message Boards are open to anyone who wants to take part, but because they are run by the official LEGO company, you'll need a LEGO ID to register and take part. The good news is that a LEGO ID is free and very easy to get.

One important point to note about the LEGO Message Boards is that they are heavily moderated. There's no lower age limit on these forums, so to make sure that the content is safe for everyone, your posts are checked before they are made public. That doesn't mean there isn't a lively discussion and a large number of participants, though. As I write this, over 50,000 people are viewing the Message Boards.

ReBRICK

ReBrick (at *rebrick.LEGO.com*) is the LEGO company's own social media platform. Aimed more at teenagers and adults than the LEGO Message Boards, ReBrick showcases the amazing array of creations that LEGO fans from around the world have made.

The idea behind ReBrick is not to store any pictures, videos, or links itself, but to provide LEGO fans with a way of bookmarking links to all that content in one place. If you've used Delicious, Pinterest, reddit, or Digg, then you'll find ReBrick very familiar. If you haven't used any of these sites, then think of ReBrick as a great resource of links to amazing LEGO content.

What you won't find on ReBrick are any official LEGO sets or sales pitches. Like much of the fan community, ReBrick concentrates on MOCs or "My Own Creations"—models designed by LEGO fans like you and me.

LEGO CUUSOO

If you have ever wanted to create a LEGO set that you can see being sold in a shop, then LEGO CUUSOO (*lego.cuusoo.com*) is the site for you. CUUSOO is originally a Japanese idea, but similar in ethos to the more widely known Kickstarter or Indiegogo. The site's basic concept is that if an idea is well supported, then it can become a reality.

LEGO CUUSOO allows you to create your own original idea and submit it to the site. You don't need to have built the idea from LEGO, or even have a 100 percent finished idea, but you do need to have a great idea that will attract attention. Once you've submitted your idea to the CUUSOO site, it is then your task to promote that idea as widely as you can.

To turn an idea into a LEGO set, the first challenge is to rally 10,000 supporters to vote for your idea on the site. Then, four times a year, the CUUSOO team will review all of the projects that have reached the 10,000 mark to see which will be made into an official LEGO set. So far, four CUUSOO sets have been released, with many more projects already under consideration or in the production process. So, what are you waiting for?

Rebrickable

The LEGO® Group supports a wide range of websites, but once you step into the fan community, there is an even wider range of content available. Rebrickable (*rebrickable.com*) is a fan site that aims to solve the dilemma that all LEGO builders have at some point in time: do I have enough bricks to build this?

Rebrickable allows you to browse a selection of individual creations with full lists of all the parts you'll need to build them. More than that, though, you can also upload a list of the official LEGO sets that you already own, and Rebrickable will tell you which models you can build with the bricks from those sets.

The Rebrickable site is a great example of a site that brings together multiple technologies developed by the LEGO fan community. By parsing the 3D CAD files created by LDraw editors and combining these with the information available at the online marketplace, bricklink.com, the site creates a whole new way to decide what to build.

Blogs and Fan Sites

The list of LEGO blogs and fan sites grows longer every day. Some, like my own at warrenelsmore.com, are related to individual people. Others, like brickshelf.com, showcase creations from thousands of fans. There are news sites, discussion sites, and everything in between.

From the long list of websites, there are a few LEGO fan sites that I visit regularly which might prove a good place to start. Firstly, there's brickset.com, which bills itself as "the top online resource for LEGO collectors worldwide." Although I certainly wouldn't disagree with that statement—it's somewhat of an understatement. Brickset has the largest and most complete database of every LEGO set ever made, as well as the ability to record your own collection. The site also showcases the latest LEGO news and set reviews, as well as hosting a lively discussion forum.

Although based in Europe, *eurobricks.com* is certainly not confined to the continent. Eurobricks is based around a huge online discussion forum, but also highlights its members' creations and product news. Eurobricks is also well known for the set reviews created by its members. In fact, the standard of reviews is now so high that they have their own "academy" to teach new reviewers the ropes.

The final site that I frequent often is The Brothers Brick (brothers-brick.com). The Brothers Brick concentrates mainly on showcasing the best creations by LEGO fans from around the world. The general standard of models shown is very high and most builders are very happy to be featured on the site.

Flickr, YouTube, Facebook, etc...

Although there are a huge number of dedicated LEGO websites, online LEGO content isn't restricted to those. Whether your favorite online experience is via Flickr, YouTube, Facebook, Twitter, or any other social media site, you can be guaranteed that LEGO fans will have a strong presence there. Just search for "LEGO."

ANCIENT WONDERS

GREAT PYRAMID OF GIZA

The Great Pyramid of Giza is the only one of the seven original wonders of the world still standing, but when you consider its size, that's not surprising. At 482 feet (147 meters) tall with sides measuring 754 feet (230 meters), it's too big to recreate fully even in LEGO® form. When complete, the pyramid would have been clad in shining white stone—very little of which remains. So, we've chosen to highlight the craftsmen finishing off the last corner of the pyramid.

Contrary to belief, the builders weren't slaves, but trained workers. Opinions vary on how many workers were needed, but it would have taken them at least ten years to complete it.

SPHINX

The great Sphinx of Giza is the largest monolithic statue in the world, standing over 240 feet (70 meters) tall. Built more than 2,500 years ago, many of its distinctive features are still very well preserved. The nose, of course, hasn't survived—historians believe it was broken off in the sixteenth century.

MINI SPHINX

The name of this national Egyptian emblem originated in Greek mythology. The Sphinx was said to guard the entrance to the city of Thebes and only granted safe passage to those who correctly answered its riddle. The mini version below is designed to be less intimidating.

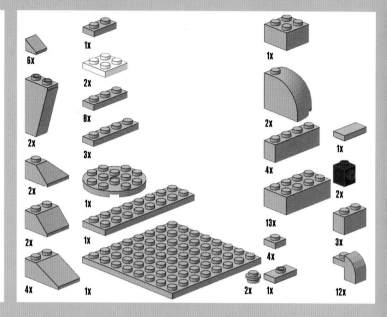

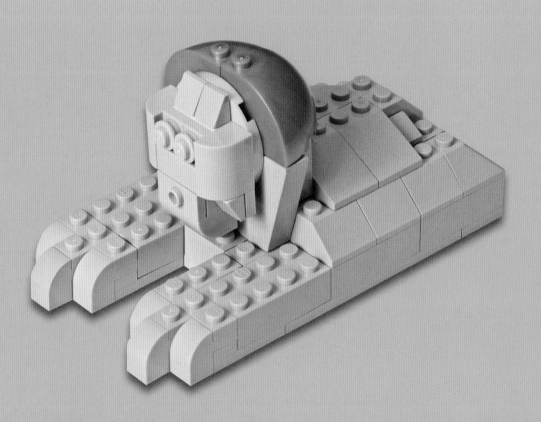

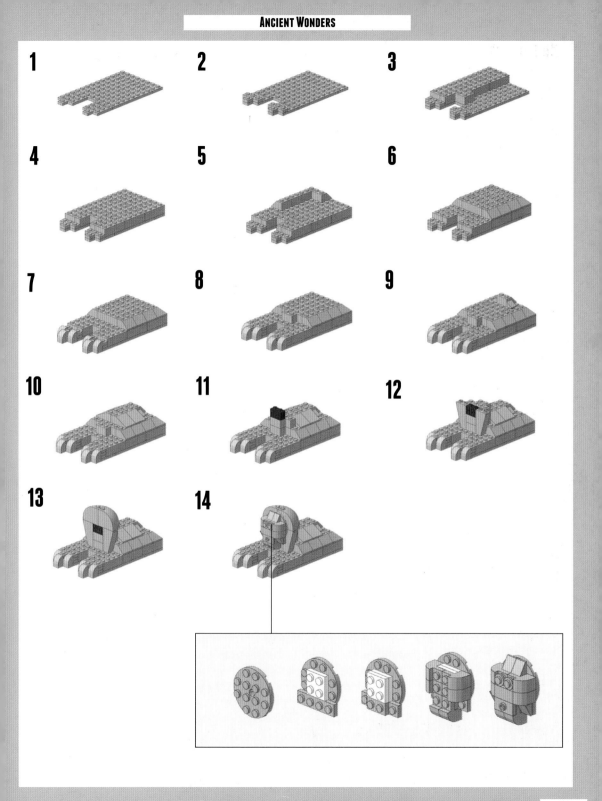

SCARAB

In ancient Egypt, the scarab was revered as a sacred creature. Today, it's known as a dung beetle. Scarabs were carved not just as hieroglyphics, but amulets, grave goods, and jewelry. Although the dung beetle would rarely grow to the size of our LEGO® model, in real life, some species of scarab grow up to 6¼ inches (160 millimeters) long, making our model life-sized.

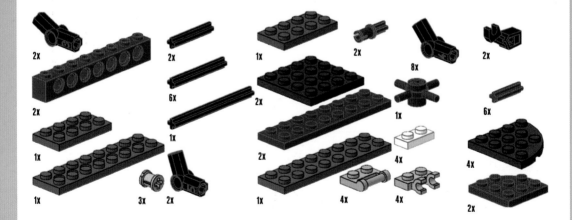

2x 2x 1x 2x 8x 2x

2x 6x 2x 1x 6x

1x 1x 2x 4x 4x

1x 3x 2x 1x 4x 4x 2x

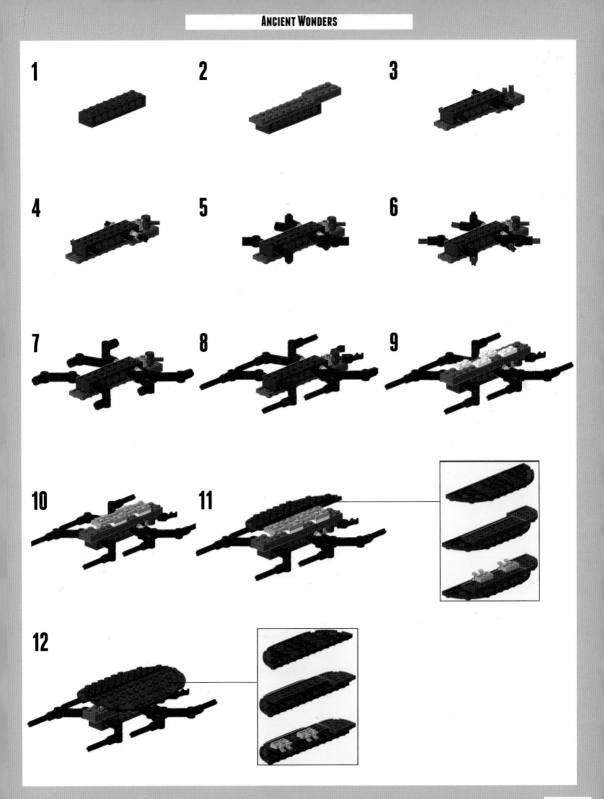

HANGING GARDENS OF BABYLON

No one really knows what the Hanging Gardens of Babylon looked like. In fact, we don't know for certain where they were located. Said to have been built by King Nebuchadnezzar II around 600 B.C., they were possibly a gift to his wife. She felt homesick for the plants of Media, so the king built her a fabulous garden, raised high on stone pillars. It was watered all year round—even in the harshest of droughts—and became a wonder of the world.

As there isn't any evidence of the real gardens, our model is based on an eighteenth-century engraving by Dutch artist Maarten van Heemskerck, with a little imagination thrown in.

TRIREME

The trireme is known as a Greek vessel, but in fact it was used all over the ancient Mediterranean. With banks of oarsmen on each side, the ships were fast and agile, and perfect for warfare. Technically, a trireme should have three rows of oars on each side, but with a LEGO® model this small, you'll just have to imagine they're there.

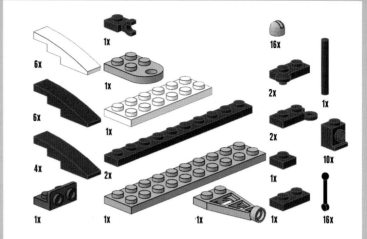

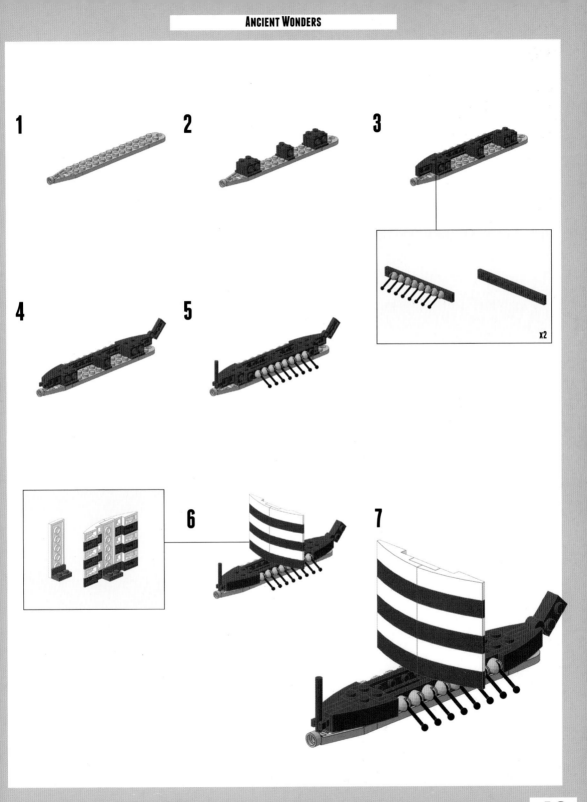

1

2

3

x2

4

5

6

7

FOUNTAIN AND TREE

Central to any queen's garden must be a fountain—especially in the hot weather conditions of the Middle East—to add movement and sound, and of course to cool the air. Our LEGO® fountain is a simple construction—the trick is to build the main part upside down to use the cones to create cascading layers. The palm tree complements the overall look perfectly.

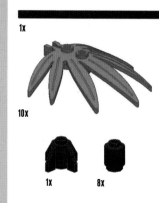

1x

10x

1x   8x

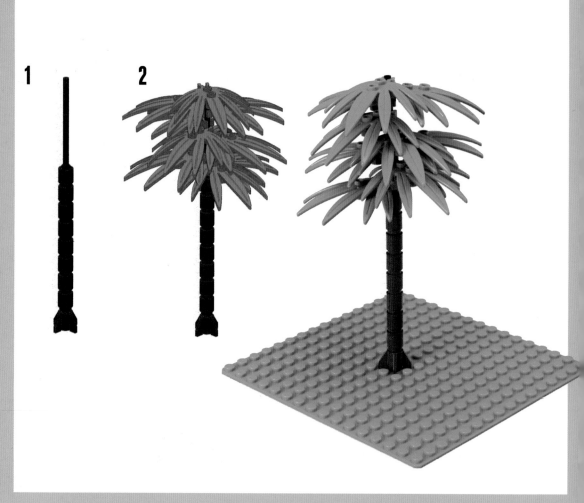

1

2

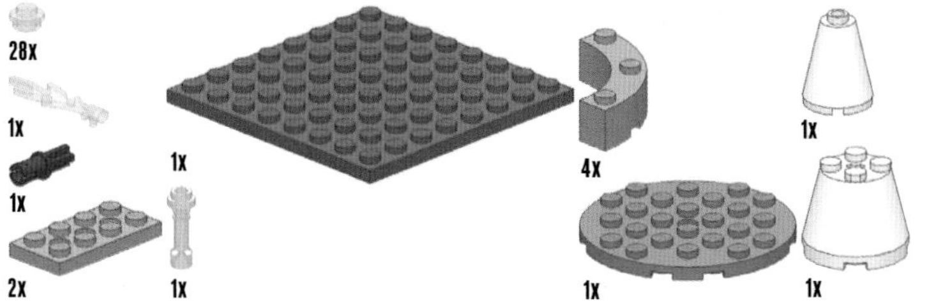

28x
1x
1x
1x
2x
1x
4x
1x
1x
1x
1x

1

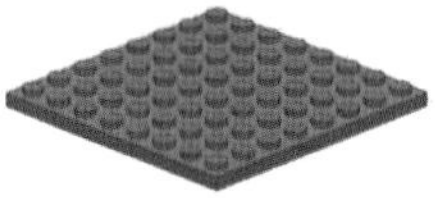

2

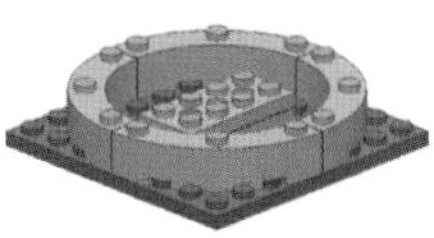

3

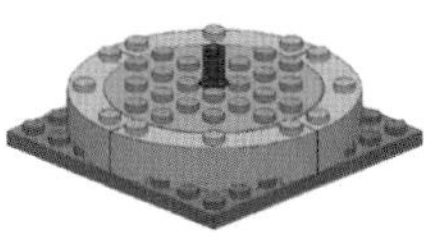

4

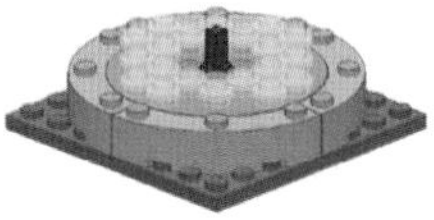

5

6

7

Zeus was the king of all the Grecian gods. The Statue of Zeus at Olympia was one of the largest ancient statues to have ever been built. At over 42 feet (13 meters) tall, it stood in its own temple which could barely contain it. It is said that the image of Zeus was inspired by a description in Homer's *Illiad*. Made from a wooden frame, with ivory and gold panels, it would have been a stunning sight even by our standards today.

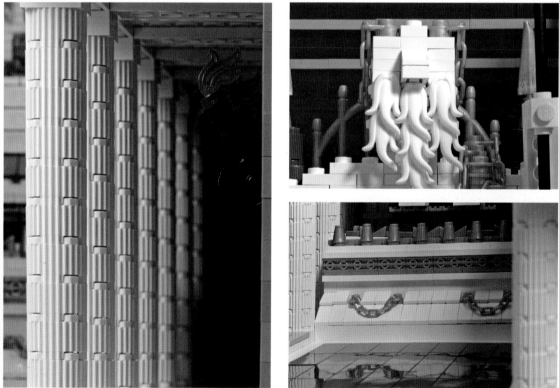

Sadly, it is believed the statue was destroyed during the Roman Empire. It was built circa 435 B.C., confirmed when archeologists found artifacts from the workshop of its original sculptor, Phidias, including a cup with "I belong to Phidias" engraved on the side.

THUNDERBOLT

You might not recognize this as a thunderbolt, but the ancient Grecians certainly would. Our thunderbolt is modeled on one seen on numerous urns from ancient Greece. Wielded by Zeus, the thunderbolt was originally a gift from Cyclops, a one-eyed monster from Greek mythology. It would have been a powerful weapon in his hands. We'll trust you to wield this thunderbolt carefully.

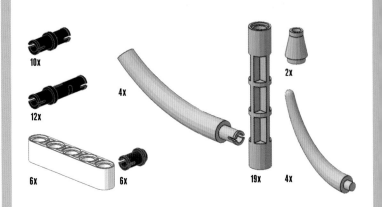

10x

12x

6x

6x

4x

19x

4x

2x

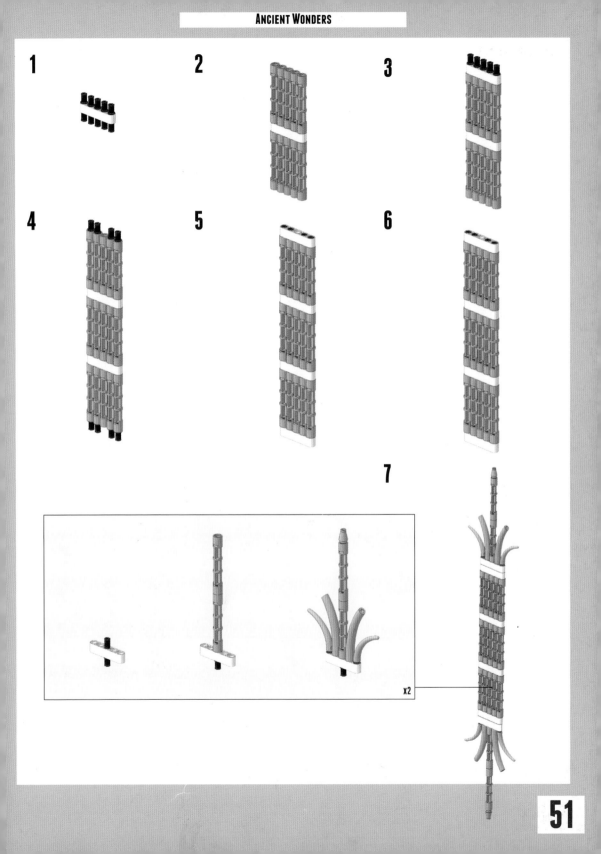

LYSICRATES MONUMENT

The Choragic Monument of Lysicrates was erected in 334 B.C. by a wealthy musical patron—just as a modern benefactor would do today. The original stands in Athens near the Acropolis, but you may be thinking it looks familiar. That's quite possible, as there are many versions of the monument around the world, stretching from Edinburgh to Sydney, to New York City.

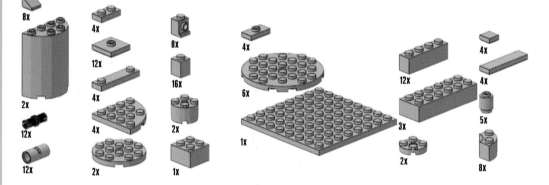

1
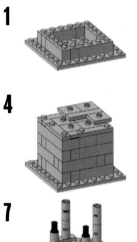

2

3

4

5

6

7

8
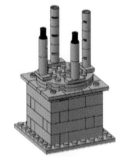

9

10

11

12

13

14

15

TEMPLE OF ARTEMIS

The Temple of Artemis depicted here is, in fact, the third temple built on this site—each one larger and grander than its predecessor. The temple was adorned with gold, and each column soared to over 60 feet (18 meters). At 450 feet (137 meters) long and 225 feet (69 meters) wide, it would not look out of place today next to a modern sports stadium.

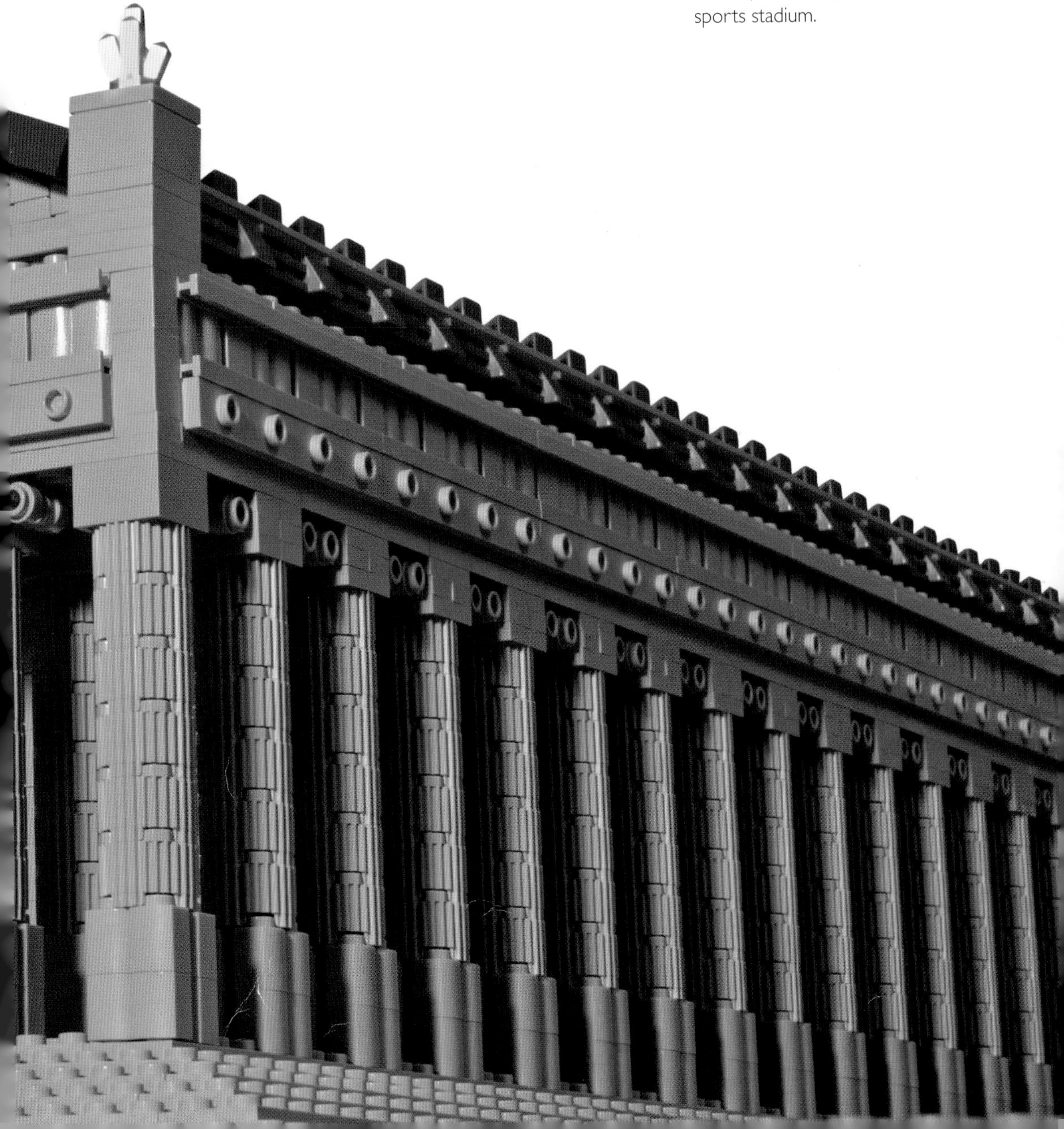

This temple was dedicated to Artemis, goddess of the hunt and daughter of Zeus. The temple survived until 400 B.C. when, like many other monuments, the stones were repurposed to build local buildings.

COLUMN CAPITAL

Each one of the 127 columns of the Temple of Artemis were alike. Made of marble, they were strong enough to hold up the huge roof, but also delicate enough to create what was regarded as the grandest of the wonders. We've used round 2x2 profile bricks to recreate the round, fluted uprights, which can be combined for a Parthenon effect.

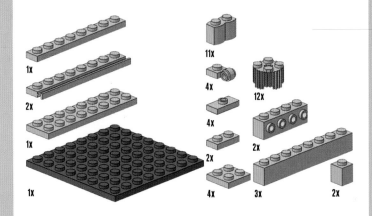

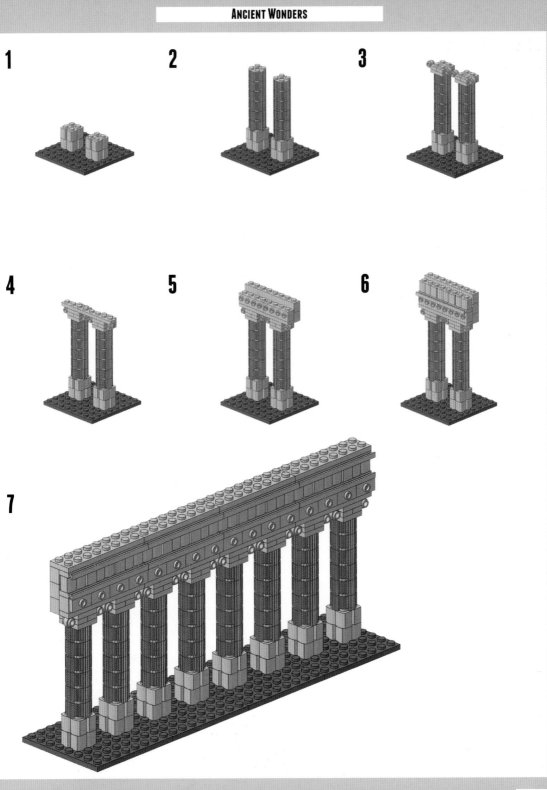

1

2

3

4

5

6

7

ALTAR

Like many temples of its time, the altar at Artemis was placed outside the temple in a separate building. In our LEGO® model, we've used fences to recreate the pillars of the altar, and jumper plates to create a short offset ledge around the outside of the altar.

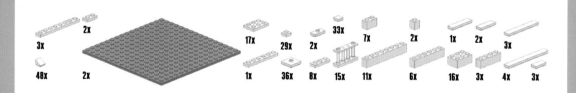

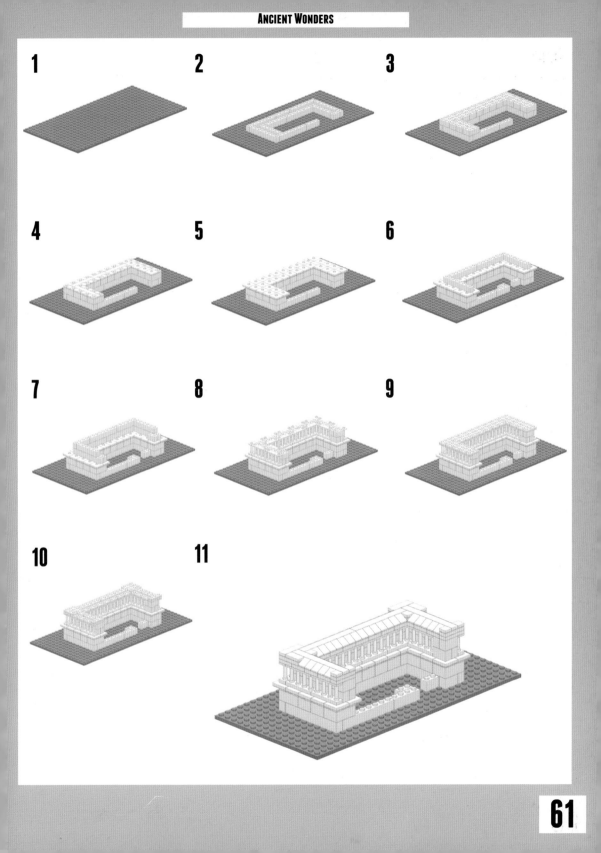

1

2

3

4

5

6

7

8

9

10

11

MAUSOLEUM OF HALICARNASSUS

The Mausoleum at Halicarnassus was built as a tribute by Artemisia for her husband (and brother) Mausolus. The best artists were commissioned from Greece, and each side of the tomb was created by a different sculptor. Although Artemisia died before it was finished, the sculptors stayed on to complete the project.

The final construction of the Mausoleum of Halicarnassus was proclaimed so beautiful that it became one of the original ancient wonders of the world. The modern-day site is now Bodrum in Turkey, where only the tomb's foundation remains.

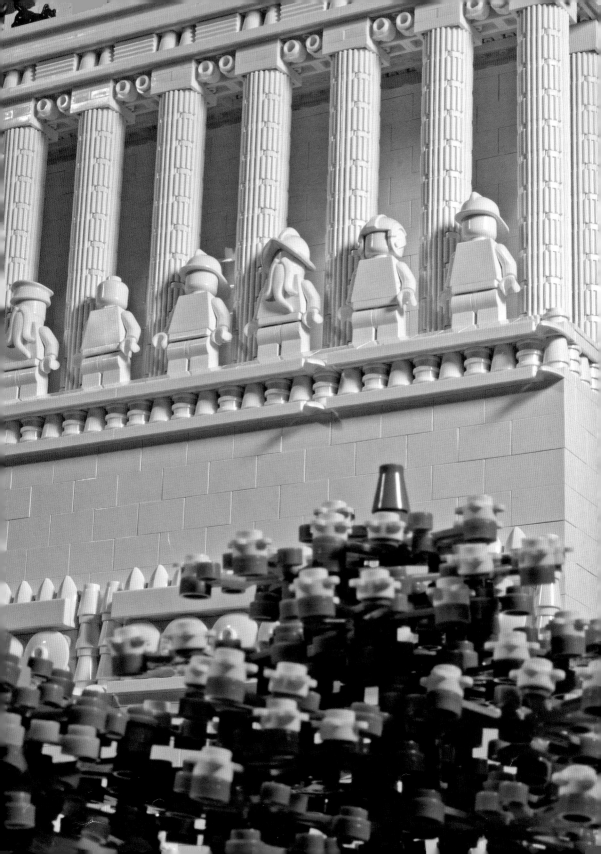

TROJAN HORSE

If at first you don't succeed, build a big wooden horse to infiltrate your enemy's city! According to the tale, during the battle for the city of Troy, after besieging the city for ten years, the Greeks pretended to sail away. They left a mighty wooden horse as a gift, which the Trojans gratefully hauled inside their walls. But little to their enemy's knowledge, the Greek warriors hid in the horse, and once night fell in the city, they crept out to let their whole army into Troy.

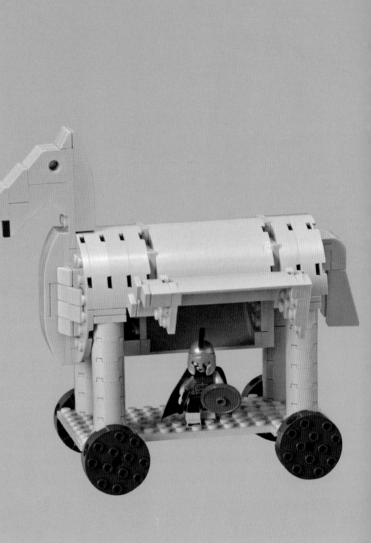

1 **2** **3**

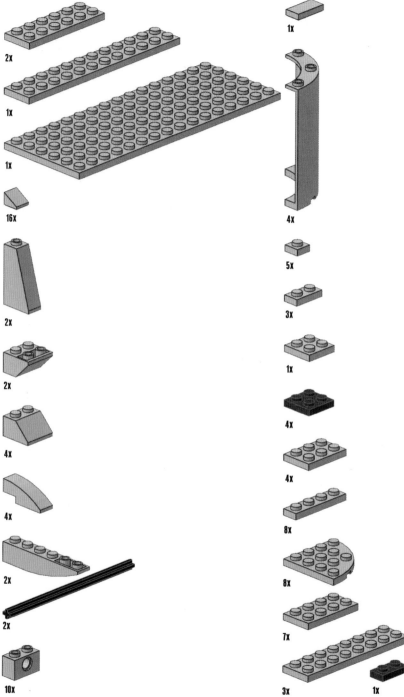

2x

1x

1x

16x

2x

2x

4x

4x

2x

2x

10x

1x

5x

3x

1x

4x

4x

8x

8x

7x

3x

4x

1x

2x

8x

12x

24x

2x

1x

4x

4x

1x

4x

6x

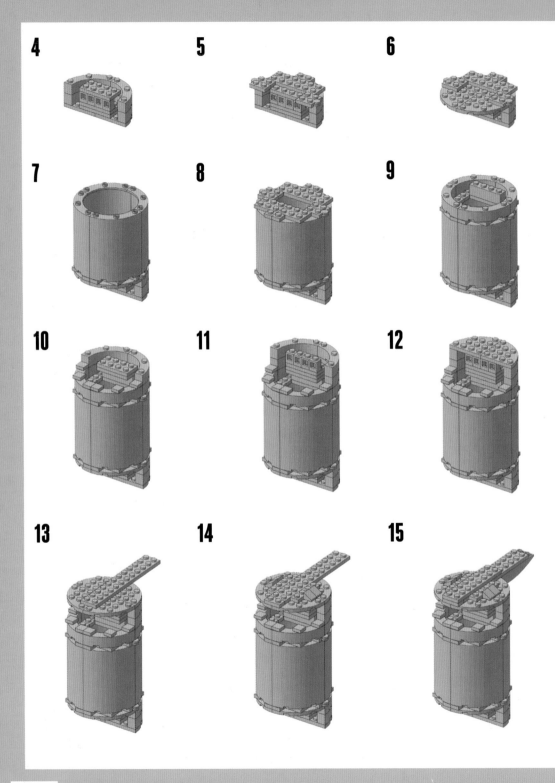

16

17

18

19

20

21

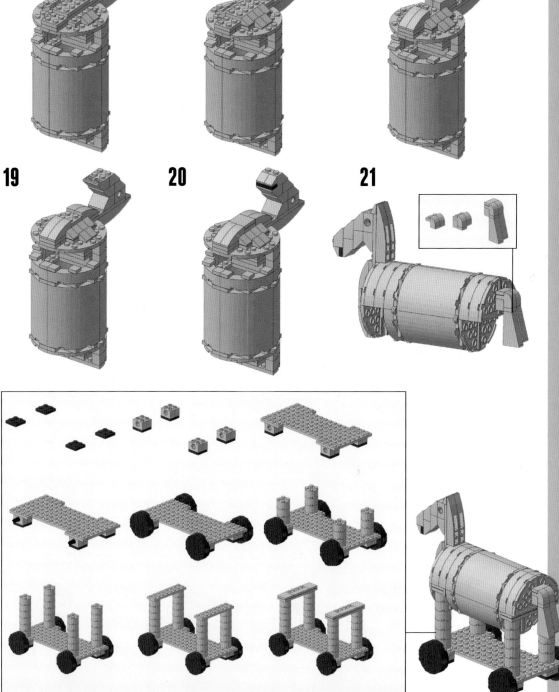

CHARIOT

The Scythians were an ancient tribe who lived in Asian steppes and would have been well known to the Greeks. They were renowned for their aggressive warriors, so a war chariot such as this would have been well used. Just make sure not to cut yourself on the knives sticking out from the axles!

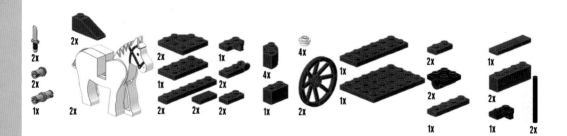

1

2

3

4

5

6

7

8

9

10

11

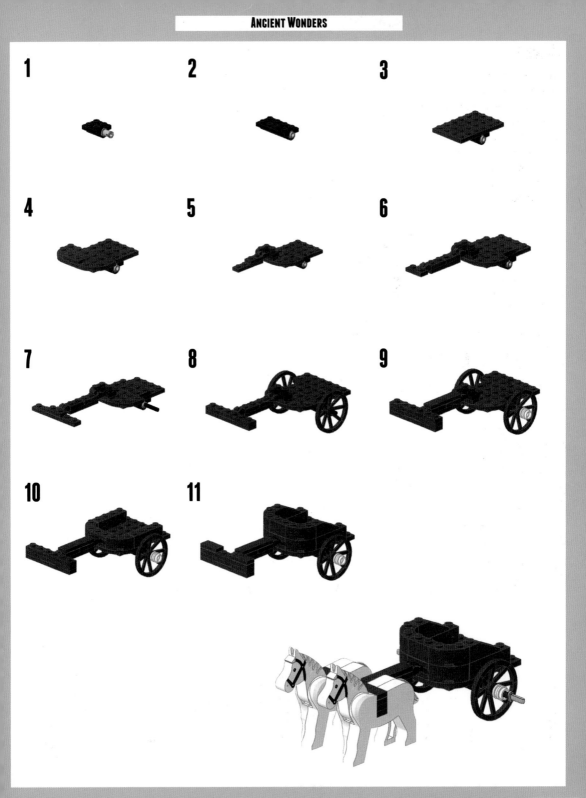

COLOSSUS OF RHODES

Although the common image of the Colossus of Rhodes is of a large statue astride the harbor entrance, sadly it's unlikely that this is how the original statue would have looked. Built around 300 B.C., it's much more likely that it would have stood to one side of the entrance—though it's still an impressive sight at 98 feet (30 meters) tall. The Colossus only survived about 50 years until an earthquake destroyed it in 226 B.C.

The ruins of the Colossus of Rhodes were so impressive that they remained a tourist attraction for more than 800 years. Architects in the late nineteenth century loved the design so much, they based New York City's Statue of Liberty on it.

MINI COLOSSUS

Our little Colossus might not be as huge as the real statue, but at least he's easier to build. Being made of LEGO® bricks means that he would easily survive the earthquake too— the disaster that toppled the real statue in 226 B.C.

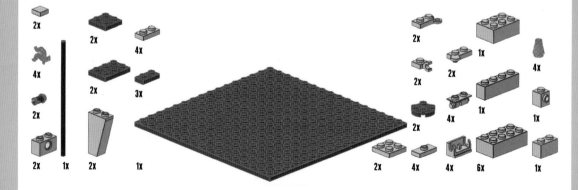

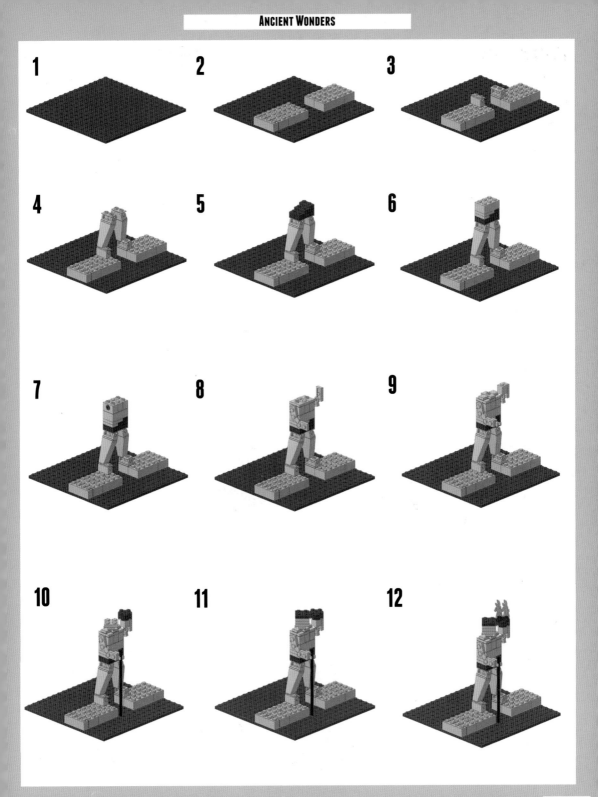

ARCHIMEDES' LEVER

Archimedes wrote about the lever: "Give me a place to stand, and I shall move the Earth with it." He was correct, as well, that to move the Earth with a lever, you would have to stand a very long way away (and you would need something very strong to rest it on). This little globe, though, shouldn't give you too much trouble.

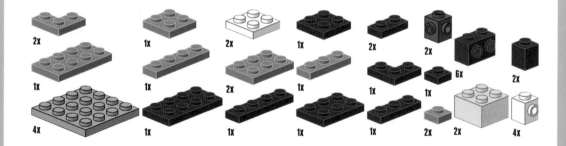

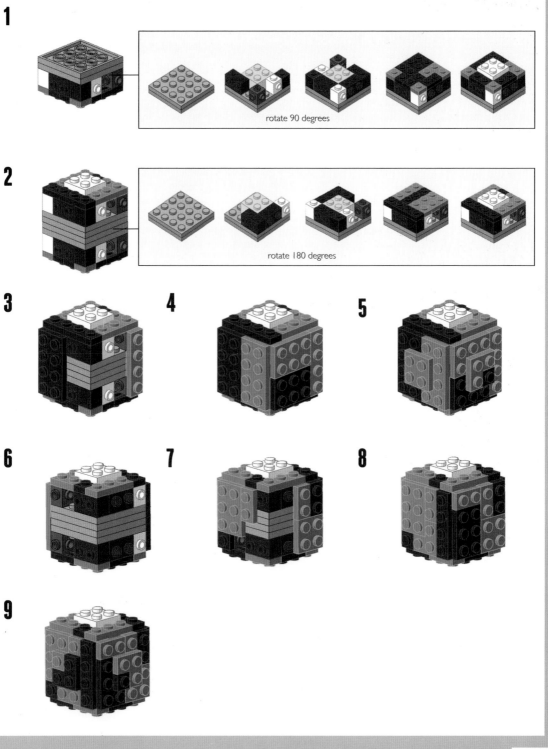

1

2

rotate 90 degrees

rotate 180 degrees

3

4

5

6

7

8

9

LIGHTHOUSE AT ALEXANDRIA

The Lighthouse of Alexandria was famous for being the tallest constructed structure on Earth for many centuries. Standing on the coastal island of Pharos, it would have safely guided Egyptian sailors into ports in around 250 B.C. Though damaged by earthquakes, the lighthouse managed to survive until 1480 when the last stones were robbed from it to build a nearby fort.

In its heyday, the lighthouse would have risen to over 400 feet (122 meters)—a similar height to the Great Pyramid—and been visible from many miles away. It was said to have cost about 800 talents, which translates to about $3 million today.

SHADUF

The shaduf is perhaps one of the most ancient methods of retrieving water, and it's still in use today. On one end of a pole is a weight, counterbalancing the weight of a bucket full of water on the other. Using a shaduf, it's possible to draw water for irrigation, drinking, or bathing with very little effort at all.

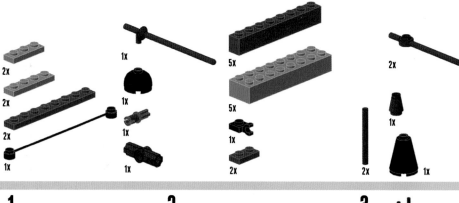

2x

2x

2x

1x

1x

1x

1x

1x

5x

5x

1x

2x

2x

1x

2x

1x

1x

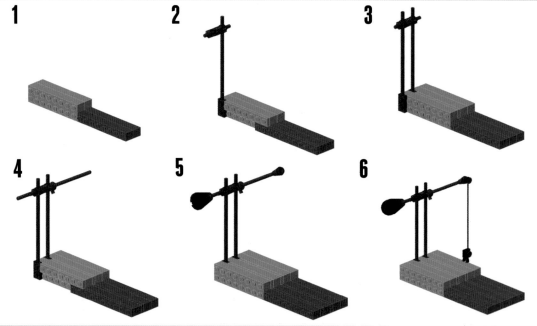

1

2

3

4

5

6

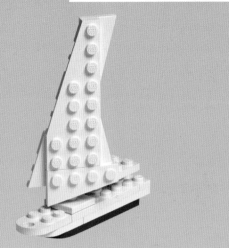

FELUCCA

The felucca is a traditional North African sailing boat with a lateen (triangular) sail. But did you know that these were also once common in San Francisco? The famous Fisherman's Wharf used to be home to a large fleet of felucca fishing boats that sailed the bay. Sadly, those are now gone, but they are still very popular on the Nile in Egypt.

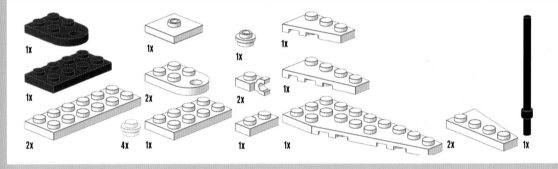

1x 1x 1x 1x
1x 2x 2x 1x
2x 4x 1x 1x 1x 2x 1x

1

2

3

4

5

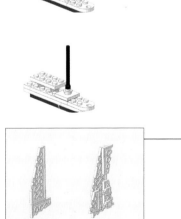

HISTORIC WONDERS

GREAT WALL OF CHINA

The Great Wall of China is often referred to as the only constructed monument visible from space. That myth isn't actually true, but this doesn't detract from the size of the wall. At over 3,500 miles (6,000 kilometers), it's certainly no garden ornament. The Great Wall was built by a series of ancient Chinese emperors between 700 B.C. and 200 B.C. to protect the country against their opponents in the north.

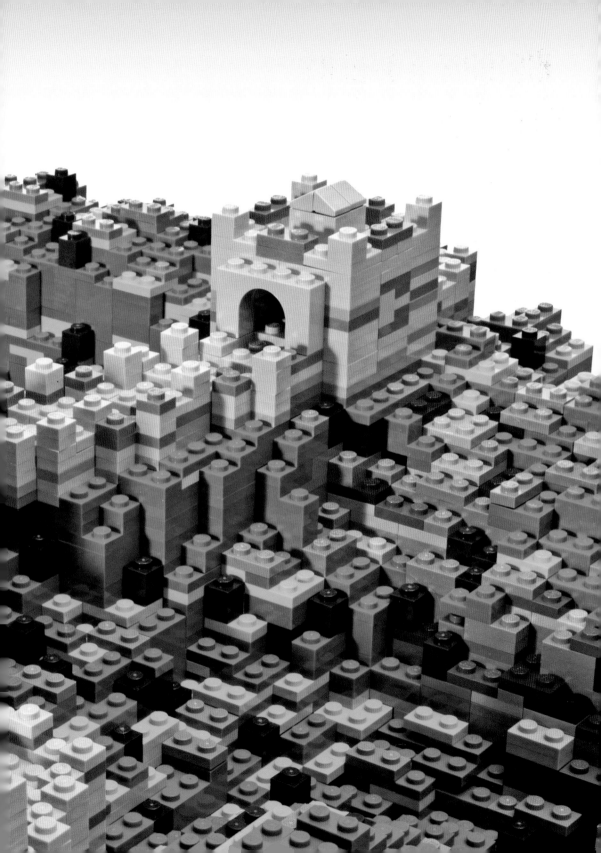

Once used as a method of border control throughout the Asian continent along the Silk Road, the Great Wall is now one of China's most famous tourist attractions, with thousands of visitors per year.

CHINESE DRAGON

The Chinese dragon dance is famous throughout the world. Supported by teams of people, the dragons dance through the streets, the dance often being a highlight of Chinese New Year celebrations. You might notice that our dragon has nine sections—and that's not by chance. The number 9 is a perfect number in Chinese society, and most dragons have at least nine sections.

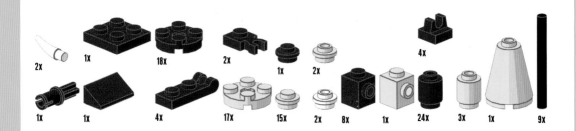

2x	1x	18x	2x	1x	2x		4x			
1x	1x	4x	17x	15x	2x	8x	1x	24x	3x	1x	9x

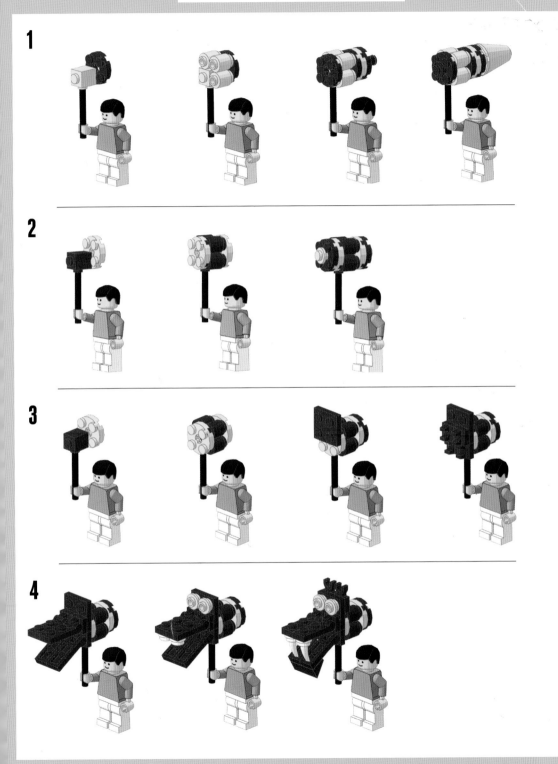

CHINESE PAGODA

While Chinese pagodas have varied in their size and design over the centuries their design is still instantly recognizable. They were originally built to house relics and sacred items but have always provided spectacular views. Although the pagodas were originally built in stone and brick, wood has since remained the most commonly used material in their construction.

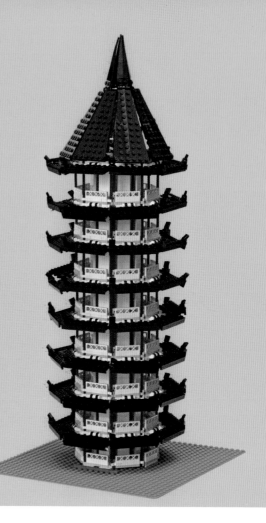

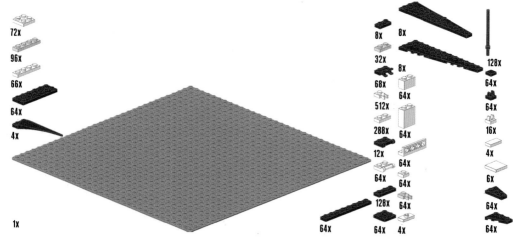

72x
96x
66x
64x
4x
1x

8x
8x
32x
8x
68x
512x
288x
12x
64x
64x
128x
64x

8x
64x
64x
64x
64x
64x
64x
4x

128x
64x
64x
16x
4x
6x
64x
64x

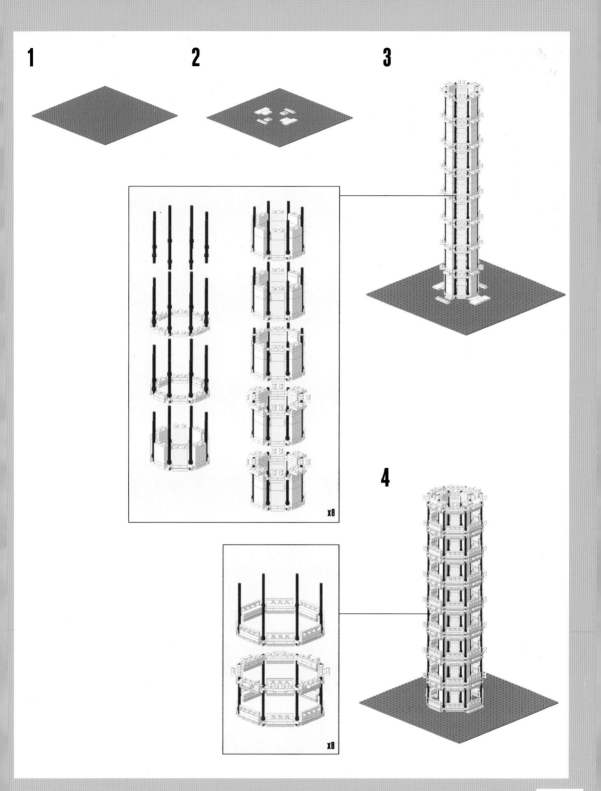

1

2

3

x8

4

x8

93

5

6

X64

x2

x2

MACHU PICCHU

Machu Picchu is situated in Peru, almost 8,000 feet (2,500 meters) above sea level. That didn't stop the Incas building this amazing city, though. Built around 1450, the city was only occupied for 100 years until the Spanish conquest came to South America. Surrounded by the Urubamba River on three sides, with steep vertical cliffs, the city was designed to be a safe haven for the Inca people. In fact, so much so that the exact location was a well-kept secret. Whether Machu Picchu was a military stronghold, a temple complex, or just a city with amazing views is still unknown. Either way, it's a globally recognized wonder.

MACHU PICCHU TRAIN

If you are lucky enough to visit Machu Picchu, then it's likely that you'll take the train at least part of the way. At its highest point, these trains reach over 14,000 feet (4000 meters). That's as tall as the Rocky Mountains, or the Alps of Europe.

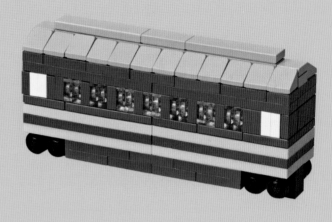

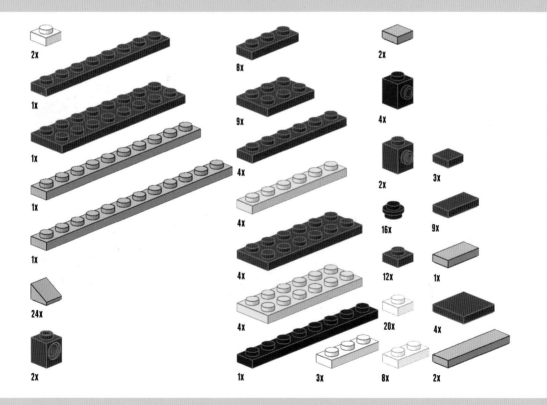

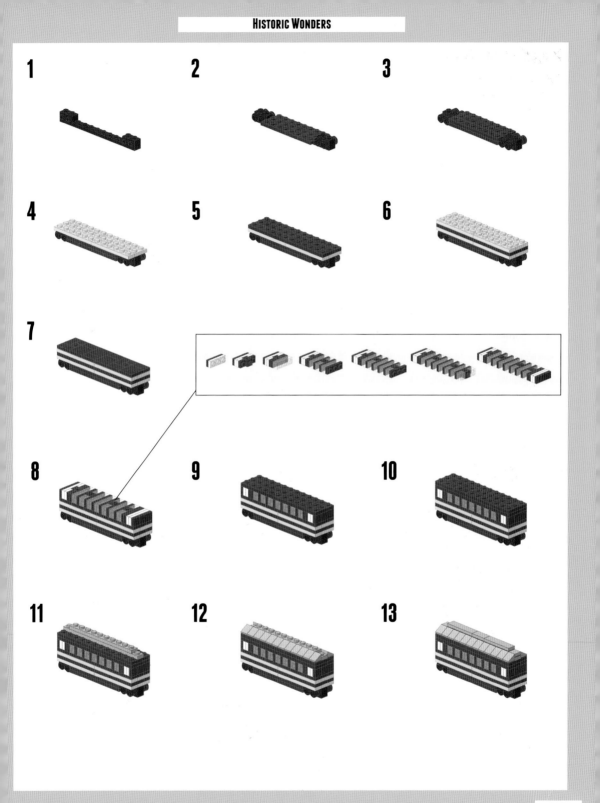

MACHU PICCHU ENGINE

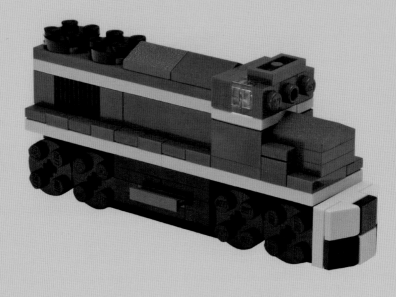

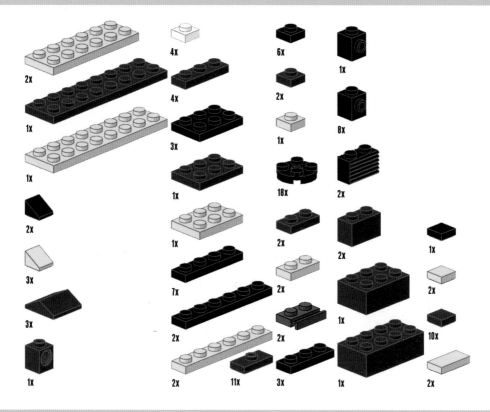

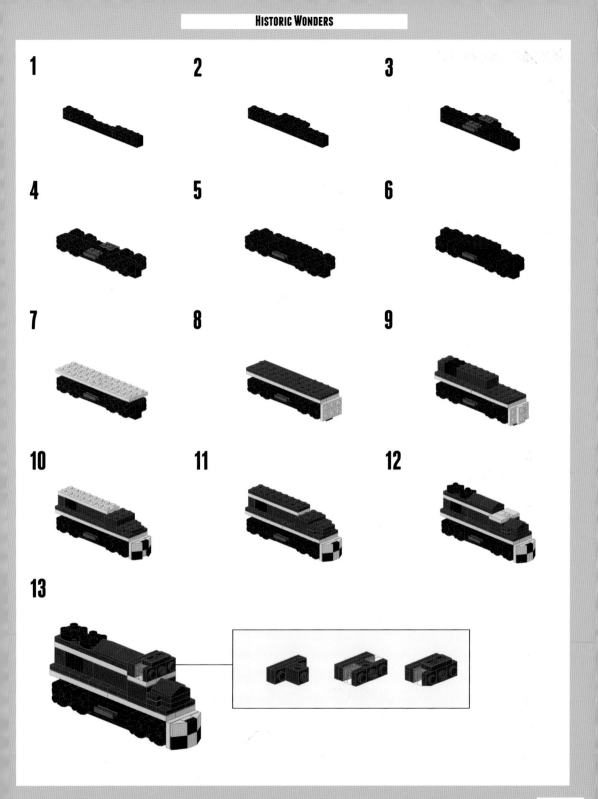

CONDOR

The condor is one of the largest flying birds in the world with a wingspan that can grow to over 10 feet (3 meters). They also live for an extremely long time—at least 50 years—and the world's oldest condor died at the grand age of 100! The Andean condor is a national symbol of Peru, and would have been a common sight to the Incas.

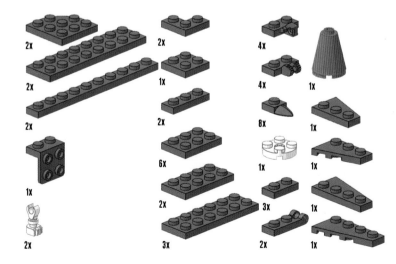

2x
2x
2x
1x
2x

2x
1x
2x
6x
2x
3x

4x
4x
8x
1x
3x
2x

1x
1x
1x
1x
1x

1

2

3

4

5

6

7

8

9

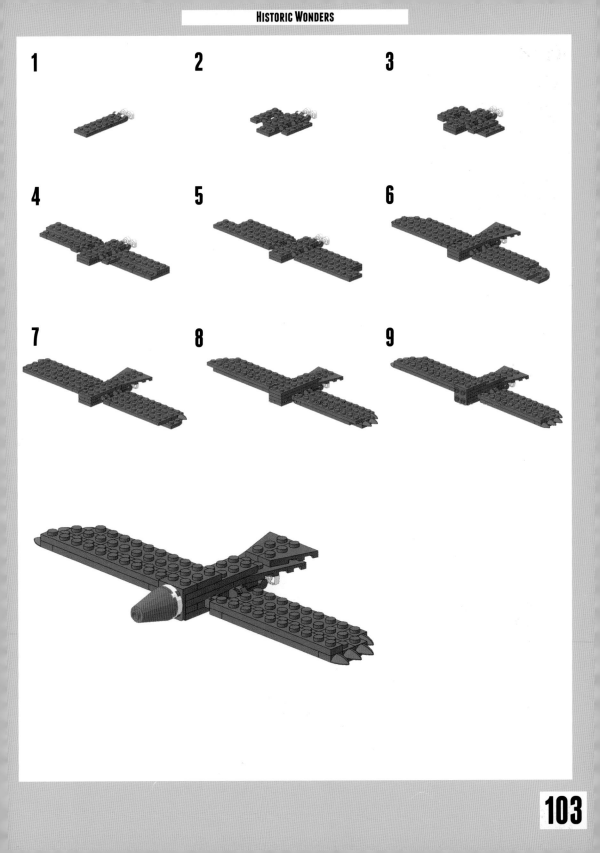

OLD LONDON BRIDGE

Old London Bridge really was a marvel. Commissioned by King Henry II, building began in 1176, and it was finally finished in 1209 by King John. Thirty-three years of building produced a bridge that was 800–900 feet (245–275 meters) long, 26 feet (eight meters) wide, and supported by 19 arches. In its place today is a concrete and steel road bridge which opened to traffic in 1973.

Each end of Old London Bridge was protected by a gatehouse, and to help recoup some of the building costs, building plots were leased out. Soon it was crammed with more than 100 shops up to seven stories high. In fact, the shops became so plentiful that many overhung the river by over six feet (two meters) and left only 12 feet (four meters) of roadway.

MEDIEVAL HOUSE

As Old London Bridge aged, the shops built along it grew larger and larger. So this little store would have been from the earlier part of the bridge's history. The beam construction can easily be seen—as can the upper stories projecting out over the ground floor.

1   **2**   **3**

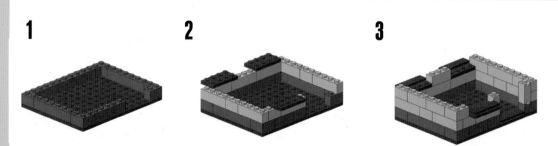

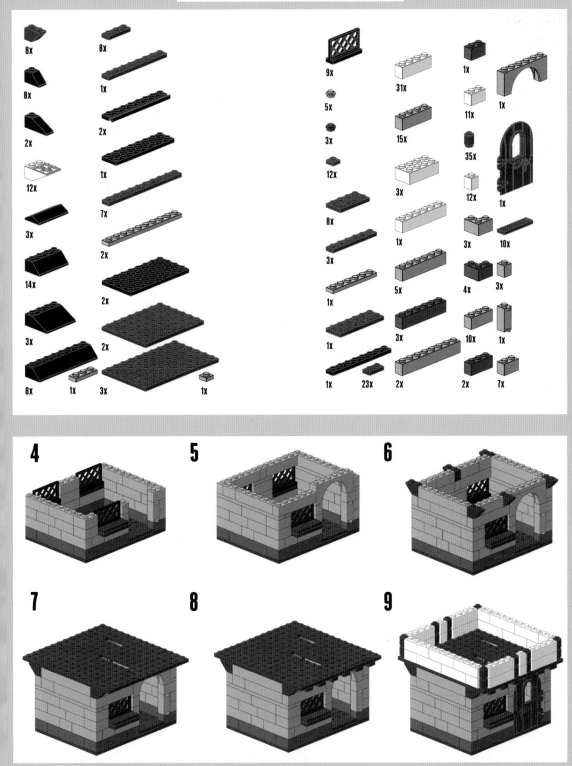

10

11

12

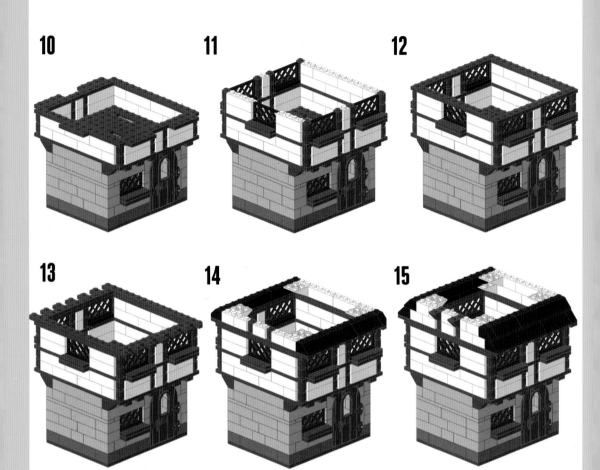

13

14

15

16

17

18

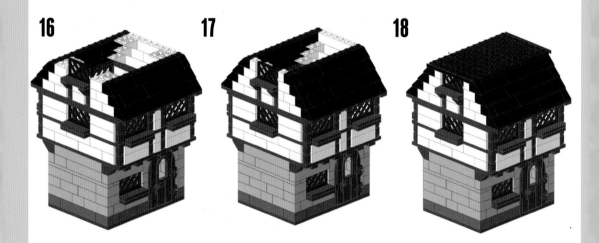

Mont Saint-Michel

Mont Saint-Michel stands off the northern coast of France, and although it's less than a third of a square mile (under one square kilometer), it's been inhabited since the Middle Ages and still has a small population who call it home. Standing at the top of the mount, is a monastery surrounded closely by houses and fortifications. The mount has long been a strategically important island and has been fought over for many years of its life. Today, however, Mont Saint-Michel is a quiet place—except, of course, for the tens of thousands of tourists who visit this World Heritage Site.

Model and photograph by Arthur Gugick.

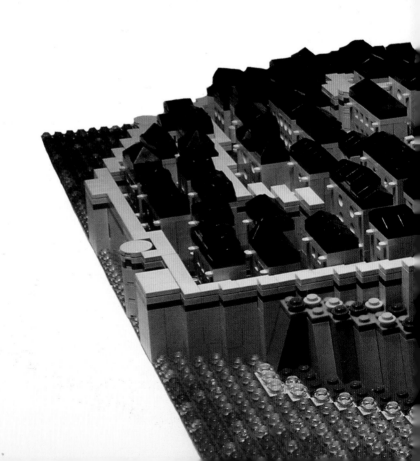

MINI MONT SAINT-MICHEL

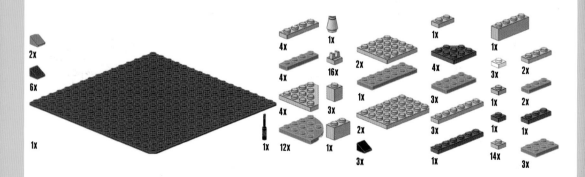

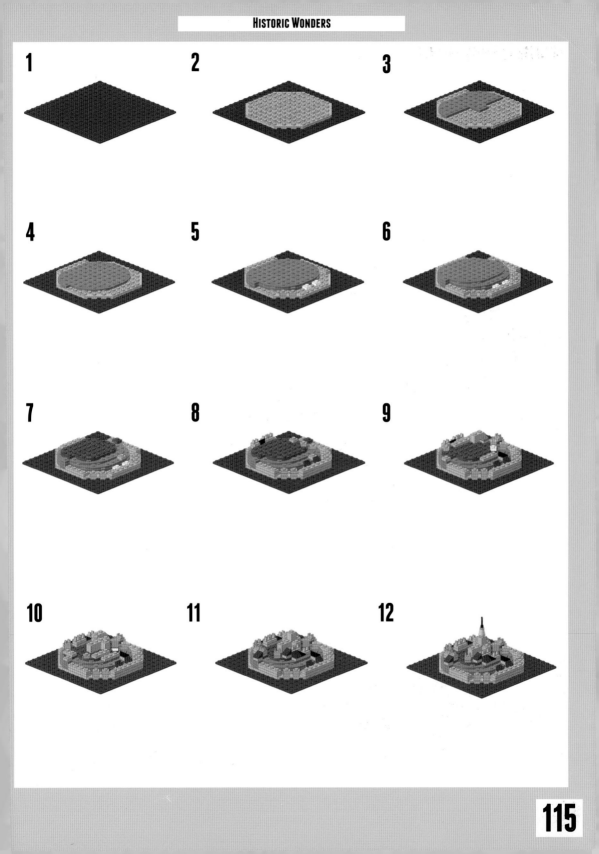

1

2

3

4

5

6

7

8

9

10

11

12

SHUTTLE BUS

The shuttle buses to Mont Saint-Michel are possibly some of the most unique in the world. The tiny island has no space for parking, so a bus literally shuttles visitors backward and forward. Nothing unusual there, but what is unique is that this bus doesn't need to turn around—it has two fronts and can be driven from both ends.

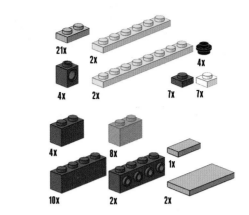

1

2

3

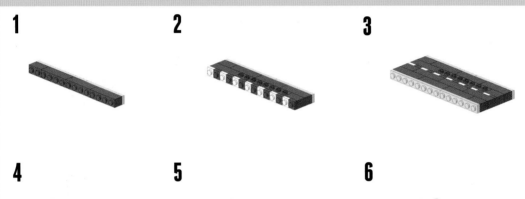

4

5

6

7

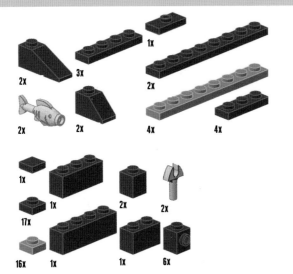

COAT OF ARMS

A coat of arms is a unique design used by many European nobles throughout the centuries. Not dissimilar from a company logo today, they are now strictly regulated in countries such as the United Kingdom so that no two are the same. This design is the coat of arms for Mont Saint-Michel. Why not try creating your own coat of arms?

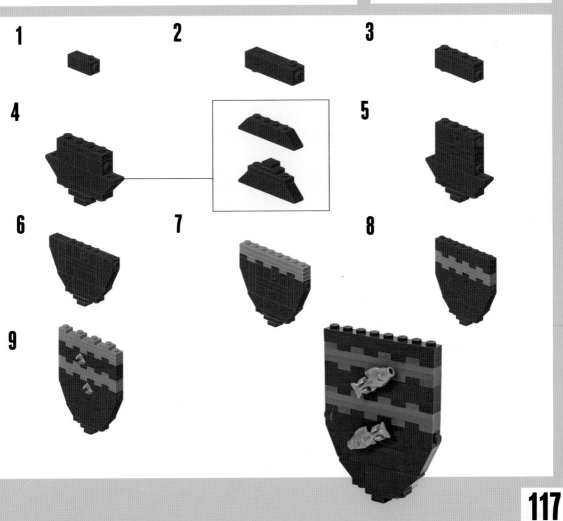

117

Petra was the capital of the ancient Nabataean kingdom, established in 168 B.C. It was Petra's position and the ability of its builders to control water that gave the Nabataeans their wealth. They controlled not only the trade routes, but also the most precious asset in the desert.

CARAVANSERAI

Traders working the routes that passed by Petra would have stopped their camel trains regularly at a caravanserai. Similar to a roadside inn or modern motel, the caravanserai would provide safe accommodation for the night. However, rather than having a parking space for your car, there were, of course, stables for camels.

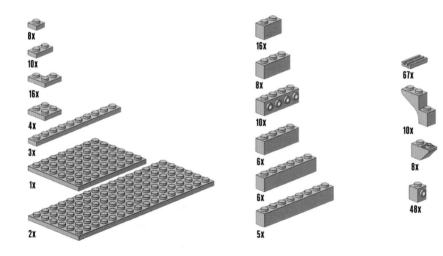

8x
10x
16x
4x
3x
1x
2x

16x
8x
10x
6x
6x
5x

67x
10x
8x
48x

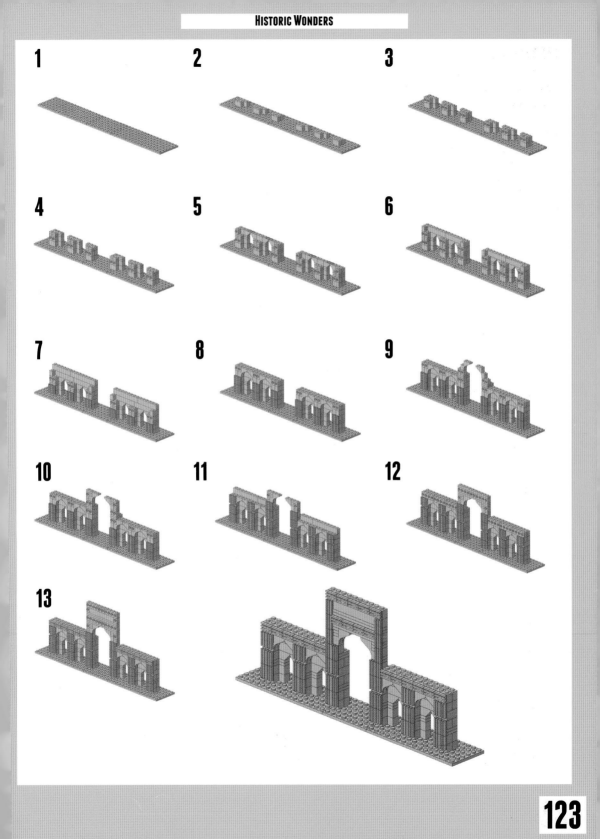

CAMEL

The camel is often called the ship of the desert. Moving across ever shifting sands, they transport countless goods and people through the Middle East every day. Did you know that one-humped camels are actually dromedaries, and those with two humps are called bactrians?

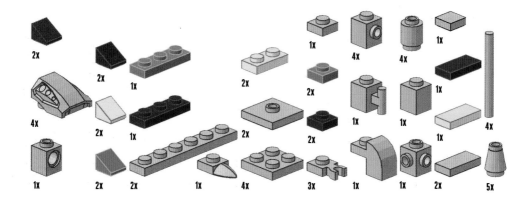

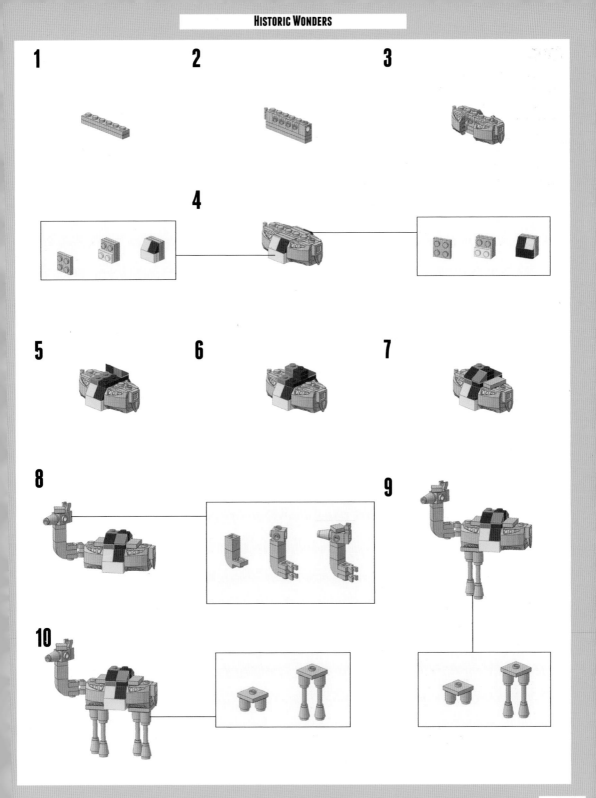

STONEHENGE

As ancient as the pyramids of Egypt, Stonehenge is one of Britain's oldest landmarks. Even though much is still unknown about the construction of the monument, scientists have recently discovered the source of the huge stones used to build the site. The stones exactly match those found in a Welsh quarry—over 140 miles (220 kilometers) away. Without any form of mechanization, stones weighing up to 50 tons each would have been moved using only basic tools and a lot of elbow grease.

New information about Stonehenge is still being discovered as archaeologists peer into its secrets. Now a World Heritage Site, this historic wonder in Wiltshire, England, attracts around a million visitors a year.

PLOUGH

As old as any of our wonders, the plough has been around as long as farmers have sown crops. Our LEGO® plough is drawn by an ox, and very few pieces are used to create it. Look out for that blade, though—it might be sharp.

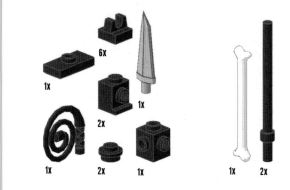

1

2

3

4

5

6

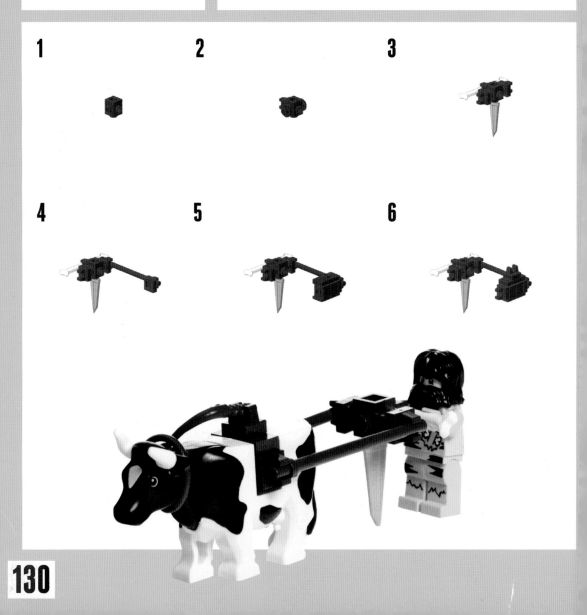

PIG PEN

If you keep animals, like our Stonehenge builders did, then you need a pen to put them in. These two simple designs show how you can build a wall or a simple fence. The wall uses round bricks to give character, and the wicker effect is created by using LEGO® robot arms between antennas.

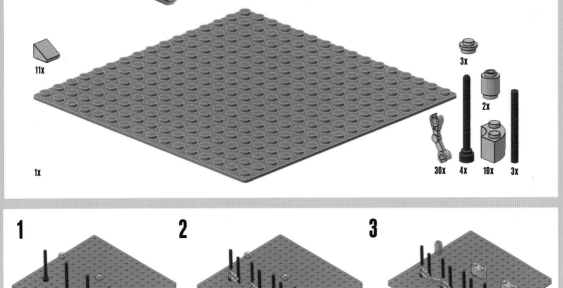

11x

3x

2x

1x

30x   4x   10x   3x

1

2

3

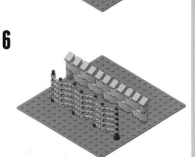

4

5

6

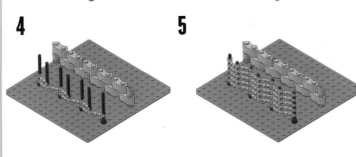

131

ROUNDHOUSE

Roundhouses like this hut were popular during the Bronze Age in parts of northern Europe. Built of dry-stone construction (with no mortar), they provided shelter to whole families. A fire would be lit in the center to keep everyone warm, and the smoke would dissipate through the thatched roof.

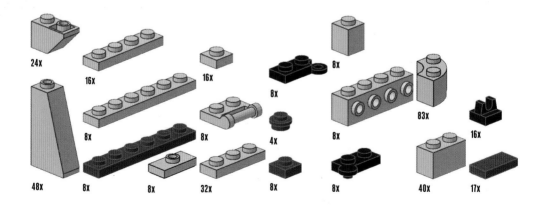

24x 16x 16x 8x 8x 83x

48x 8x 8x 32x 4x 8x 8x 40x 16x 17x

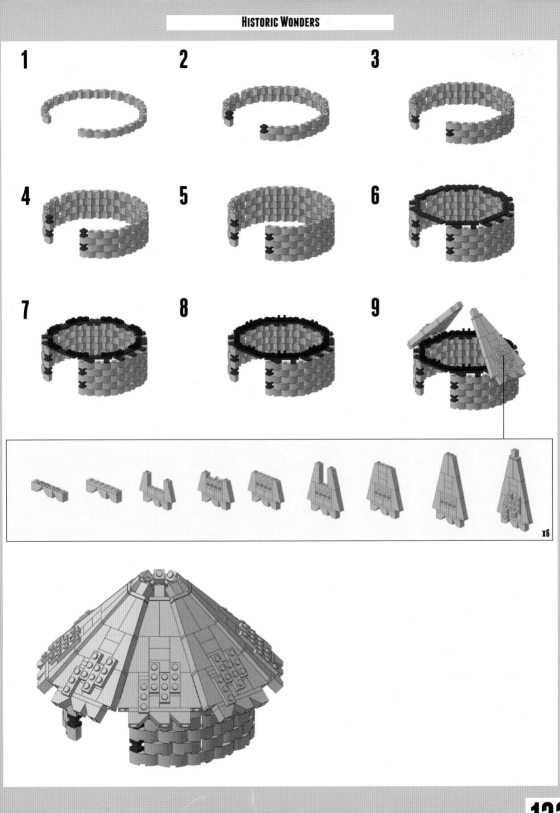

ANGKOR WAT

Cambodia's Angkor Wat is simply the biggest religious monument in the world, though perhaps big doesn't do it justice. The outer wall encloses 203 acres (820, 000 square meters) and even that is surrounded by a 570-feet- (175-meters-) wide moat. Not only is the site vast, but each temple is ornately carved with outstanding bas-relief friezes reflecting Hindu epics and historical scenes. Originally built as a Hindu temple in the twelfth century, Angkor Wat became a Buddhist temple at the end of the thirteenth century. Today, Angkor Wat is a World Heritage Site and a major tourist destination.

TEMPLE

The temples of Angkor Wat stretch over a huge area, but why not build a mini temple of your own? Re-creating the intricate nature of the temples is difficult at this scale, so our model uses differing shades of gray to represent the individual features of the dome.

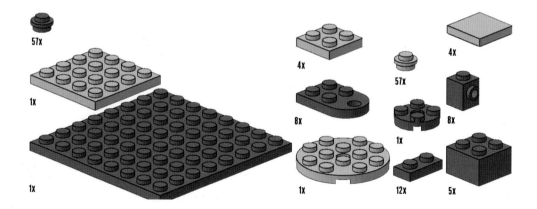

1

2

3

4

5

6

7

8

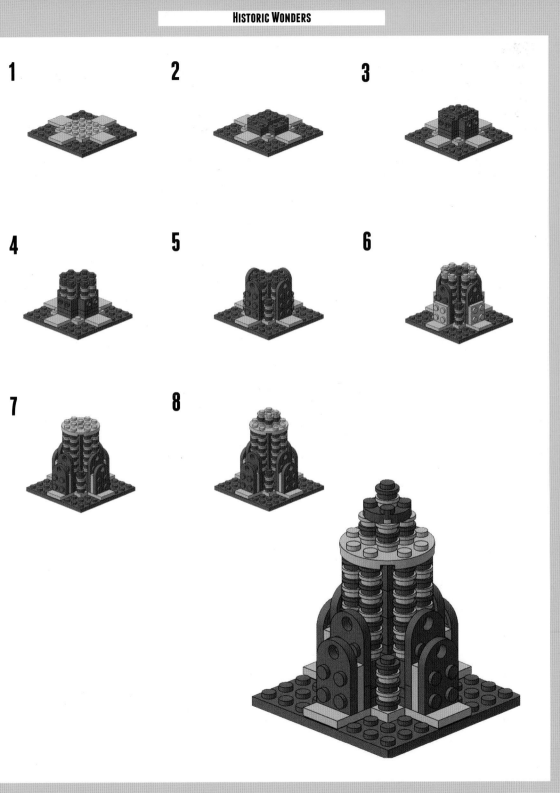

Tuk Tuk

The tuk tuk is a common sight in Cambodia and much of Southeast Asia. A cross between a motorcycle and a small car, they are the main form of public transportation in many areas. With a top speed of only 30 miles per hour, they might not be as fast as a taxi, but the three-wheeled design gives great maneuverability.

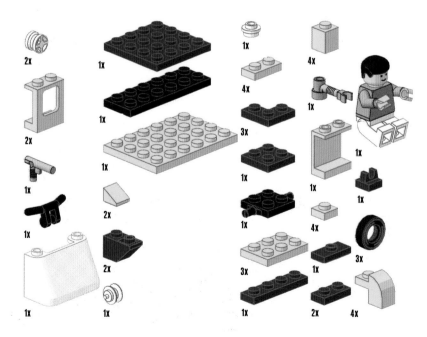

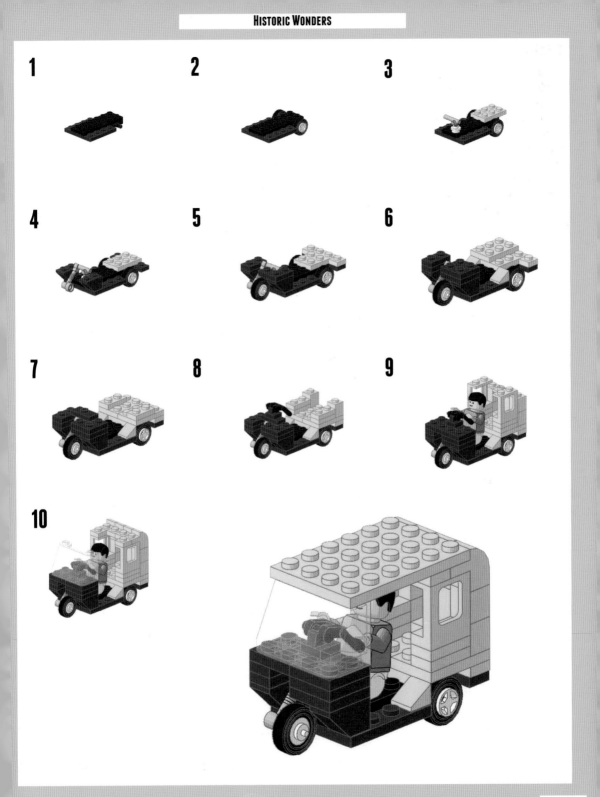

MODERN WONDERS

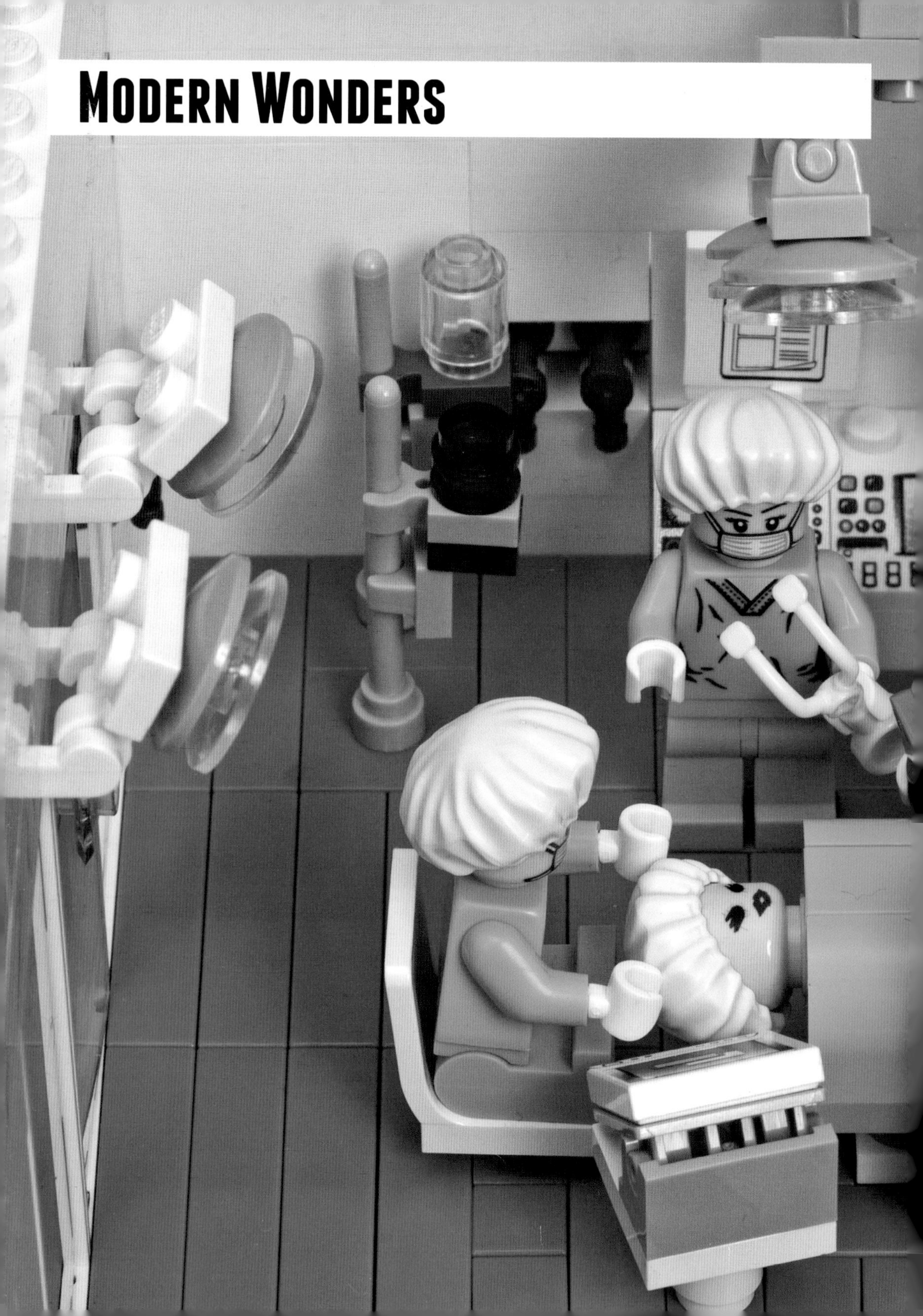

MODERN MEDICINE

Modern medicine has increased our life span and populations. Complex operations are performed in operating theaters, which originally had rows of tiered seating for students to watch surgeons at work. Today, operating theaters are kept highly sterile to help prevent infections, and only the experts are present. As seen here, standard operating theater equipment includes the table, specialized lighting, X-ray machine, and heart and blood pressure monitors.

Medical science has advanced greatly. With the introduction of antibiotics and modern techniques, what were once life-threatening conditions are now regularly treated in a hospital. If a LEGO® minifig is injured though, it's a simple case of replacing the right part.

SYRINGE

You don't need to be scared of needles with this LEGO® syringe. LEGO parts might be painful to stand on, but thankfully the tip of this syringe isn't that sharp. We've used transparent red bricks to simulate the contents of the syringe, but you could use any color.

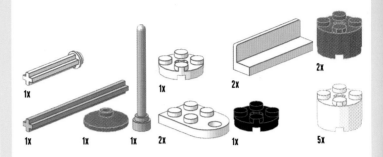

1x   1x   2x   2x

1x   1x   1x   2x   1x   5x

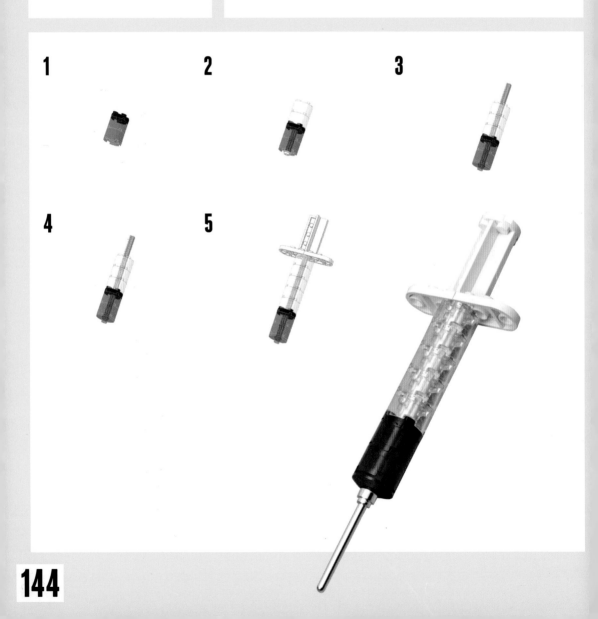

1

2

3

4

5

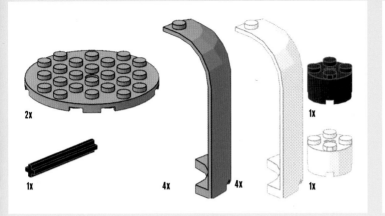

2x

1x

4x

4x

1x

1x

ANTIBIOTICS

This isn't an easy pill to swallow! Modern medicines have changed the lives of millions of people worldwide. From a simple headache cure to complex life-changing treatments, many medicines can be delivered in a simple capsule form such as this. Just remember to follow the prescription until the course is completed.

1

2

3

4

5

PANAMA CANAL

Now 100 years old, the Panama Canal is considered by many to be one of the greatest engineering feats of all time. A 48-mile (77-kilometer) canal connecting the Atlantic to the Pacific, its locks move huge ships up and down 85 feet (26 meters) from sea level. By shortening the journey from Asia to America's east coast, it provides a key route for international shipping.

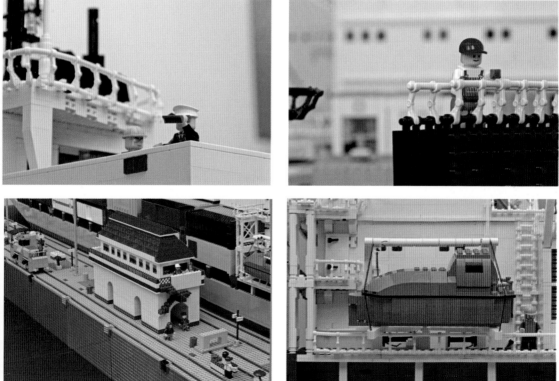

The construction of the Panama Canal began at the end of the seventeenth century but was hindered by difficult geographical conditions. The subsequent discovery of gold in California led to the construction of the Panama Railway, and then the completion of the canal at the beginning of the twentieth century.

TUG TRAIN

The ships in the Panama Canal are so large and the locks so small that special measures are needed to control the traffic. These "mules" are purpose-built trains that manage the mooring lines of the ships as they pass. The largest ships need eight mules to control their sideways motion and braking.

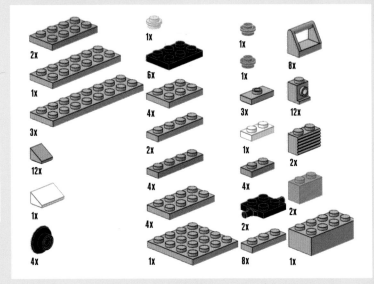

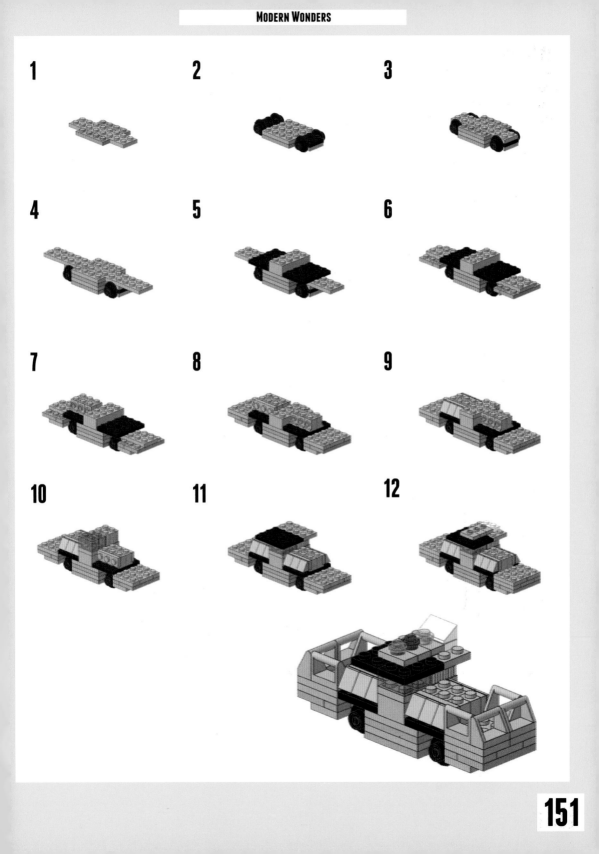

SHIPPING CONTAINER

Shipping containers have revolutionized goods transport and trade throughout the world. It's estimated that there are over 17 million containers in circulation today, shipping every type of product from one side of the world to another. This model is a tank container, which moves gases, liquids, or powders.

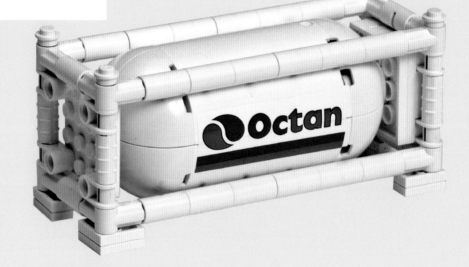

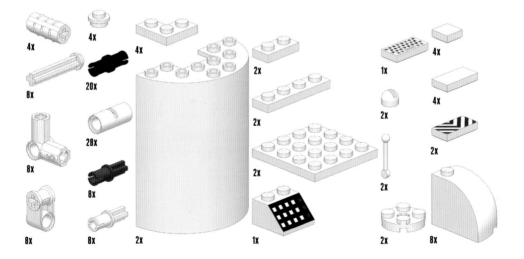

4x
4x
4x
2x
1x
4x

8x
20x
2x
4x

8x
28x
2x
2x

8x
2x
2x
2x

8x
8x
2x
1x
2x
8x

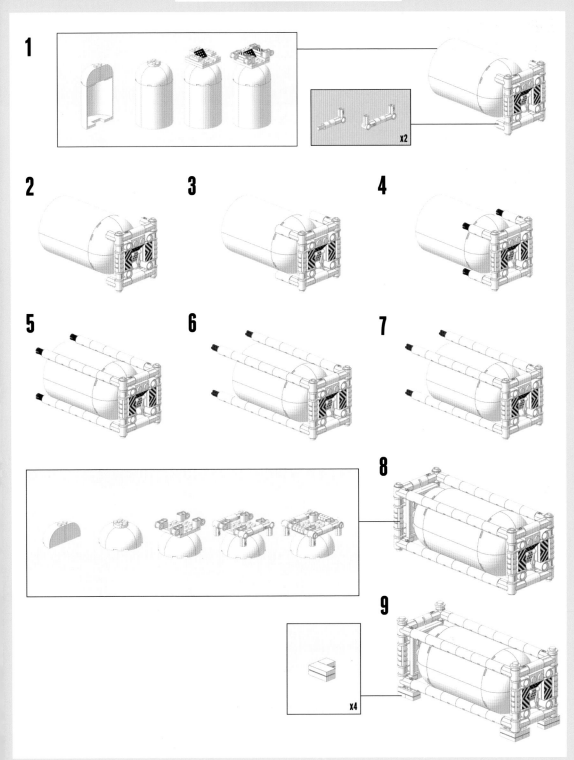

MOUNT RUSHMORE

Mount Rushmore National Memorial in the Black Hills of South Dakota depicts four American presidents and was built by sculptor Gutzon Borglum and finished in 1941, shortly after his death. Today Mount Rushmore and nearby Crazy Horse Memorial are visited by millions every year.

HOOVER DAM

The Hoover Dam, like Mount Rushmore, was also completed in 1941. This modern wonder of the American West is truly massive. It took five years to build, and over three million cubic yards (two and a half million cubic meters) of concrete were poured into the Dam alone. That's enough concrete to build a two-lane road right across the United States. Sadly, 112 people died during the building of the Hoover Dam.

Today, the Hoover Dam has two tasks. Not only does it control the mighty Colorado River, but it also powers much of Las Vegas and Los Angeles, generating 2,000 megawatts of clean hydroelectric energy.

BATTERY

The Hoover Dam isn't the only provider of power—the technology underpinning almost all modern gadgets is the humble battery. Or perhaps not so humble. Though you'll probably recognize these alkaline batteries, modern gadgets use rechargeable nickel cadmium, nickel metal hydride, and lithium ion batteries. With the increased popularity of electric vehicles, battery technology is now evolving on a constant basis.

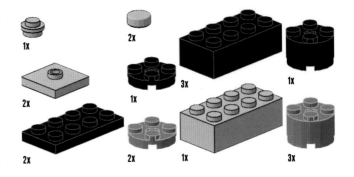

1x 2x 3x 1x
2x 1x 1x
2x 2x 1x 3x

1

2

3

LIGHT BULB

The light bulb was invented in the early 1800s, although it wasn't until 1879 that it was popularized by Thomas Edison. The first light bulbs used carbonized bamboo as a filament and lasted for only 600 hours. Now, the incandescent lamp is being phased out, replaced by more efficient LED and fluorescent lamps.

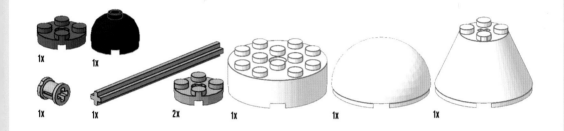

1x   1x   1x   2x   1x   1x   1x

1

2

3

4

Wind Turbine

While windmills have been a common sight for centuries, it's only recently that wind farms have been used to harness the power of the wind to generate electricity. Our model wind turbine doesn't generate any power though—it cheats by using a motor to drive the blades around.

1

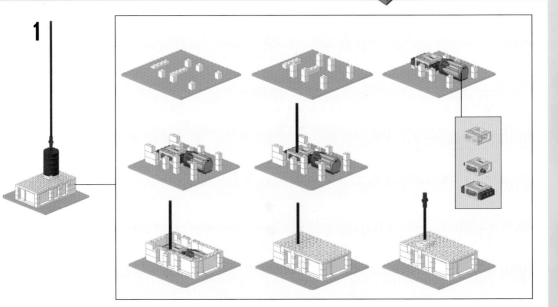

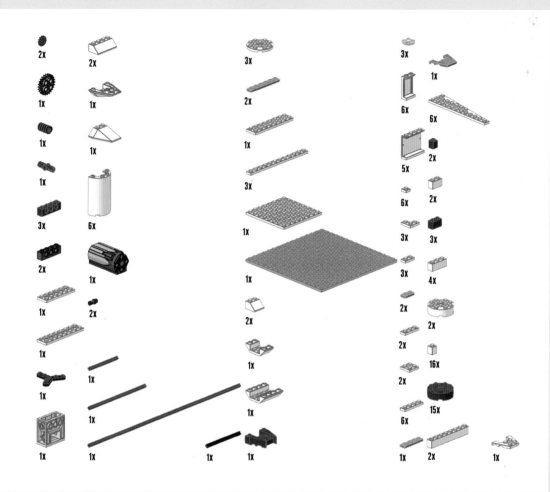

2x 1x 1x 1x 3x 2x 1x 1x 1x 1x 1x

2x 1x 1x 6x 1x 2x

3x 2x 1x 3x 1x 1x 2x 1x 1x 1x 1x

3x 1x 6x 5x 6x 3x 3x 2x 2x 2x 6x 1x

1x 6x 2x 2x 3x 4x 2x 16x 15x 2x 1x

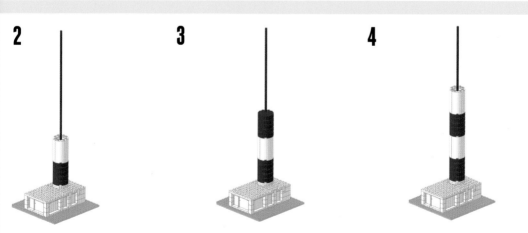

2   **3**   **4**

5

6

7

8

9

10

11

12

13

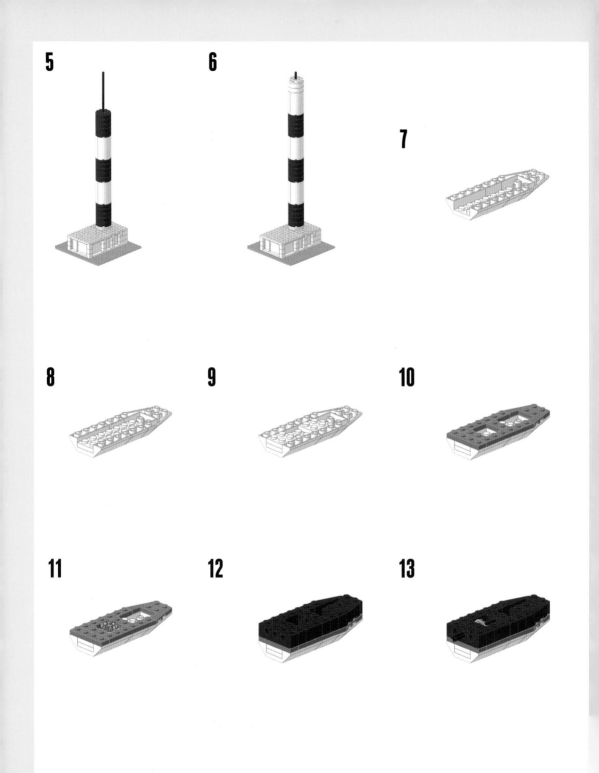

14

15

16

17

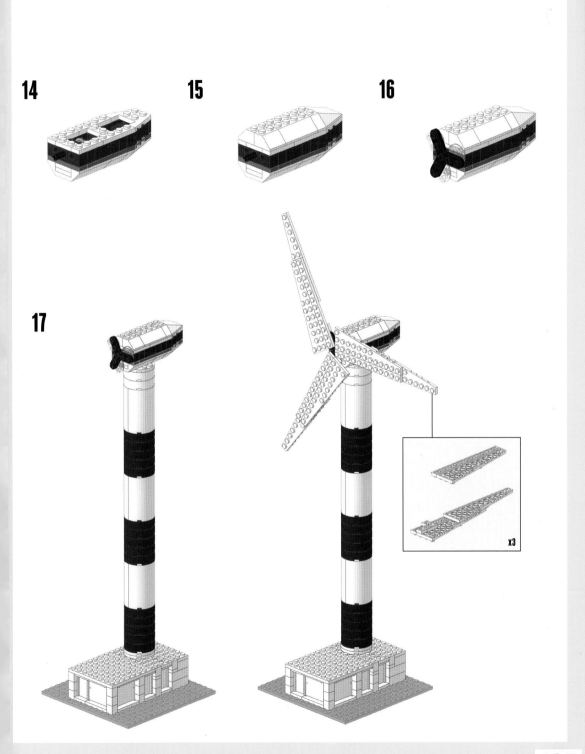

x3

MODERN COMMUNICATION

Although printing was invented in China around 600 A.D., it wasn't until Johannes Gutenberg invented his movable type in 1450 that printing became affordable. Each letter (or group of letters) was engraved onto a metal block made of a special alloy. By arranging these blocks in the right order, it was possible to lay up a page quickly and easily in order to print multiple copies. The invention of this "movable type" revolutionized the distribution of knowledge worldwide. Less than 50 years after Gutenberg's death, half a million books had already been produced.

Tv Camera

If you've watched any "breaking news" broadcasts, the chances are that the footage came from an Electronic News-Gathering (ENG) camera like this. The ENG cameras have become smaller over the years, but the shoulder-mounted format has remained popular. It's stable, easy to hold, and difficult to miss.

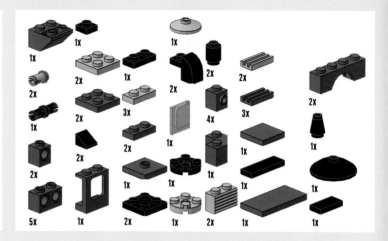

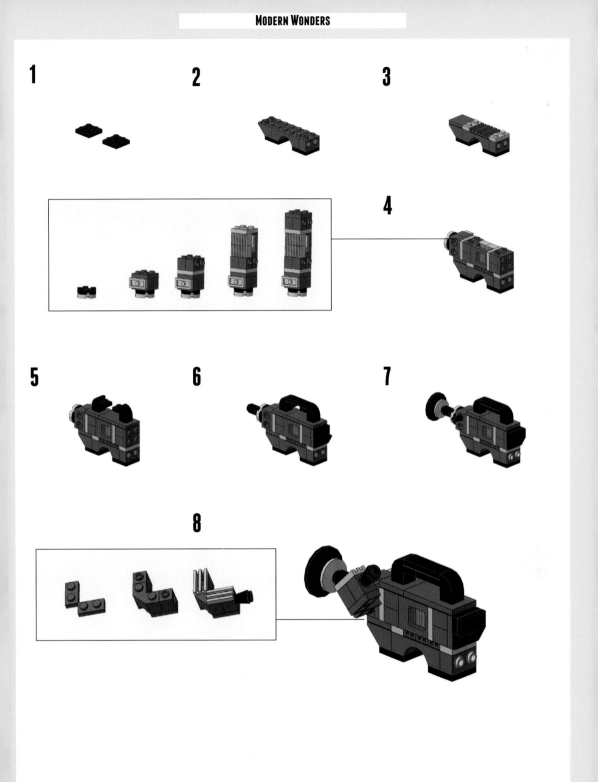

RADIO

Radio broadcasting has existed for more than 100 years. This microphone is famous for being used by the British Broadcasting Corporation (BBC) through many of its early transmissions. Even though many modern-day microphones might look different, take a look at the icon on your computer screen or smartphone. That iconic shape is still in use today.

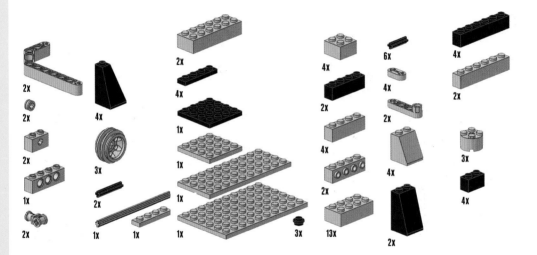

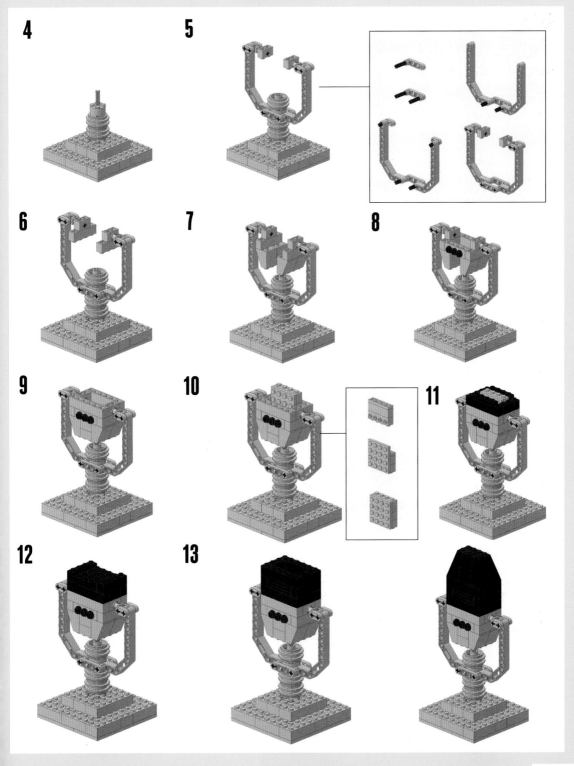

171

TRANSPORTATION

Few inventions have been credited with making the world a smaller place. Modern aviation is one of those inventions. In less than 100 years, a global infrastructure of airplanes and airports has brought us all closer together. At any one time, tens of thousands of planes are in the air transporting both goods and people to every country in the world.

Large airports cover thousands of acres, so our LEGO® model is based on a small city airport. Even at LEGO minifig scale, an accurate model of a global "hub" airport would be pretty large.

AIRPORT STEPS

Whether they're graced by bejeweled royalty or glitzy celebrities, steps are an icon of airport glamour. Roll out the red carpet, your jet-setting LEGO® minifig has arrived! Of course, most modern western airports don't use these anymore, but they are still found everywhere else and add a touch of vintage whimsy to the airport model.

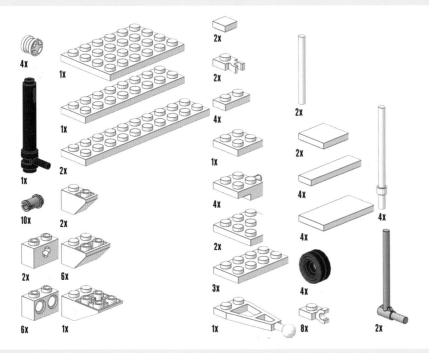

4x

1x

1x

2x

1x

10x

2x

2x

6x

6x

1x

2x

2x

4x

1x

4x

2x

3x

1x

2x

2x

4x

2x

4x

4x

8x

2x

2x

4x

4x

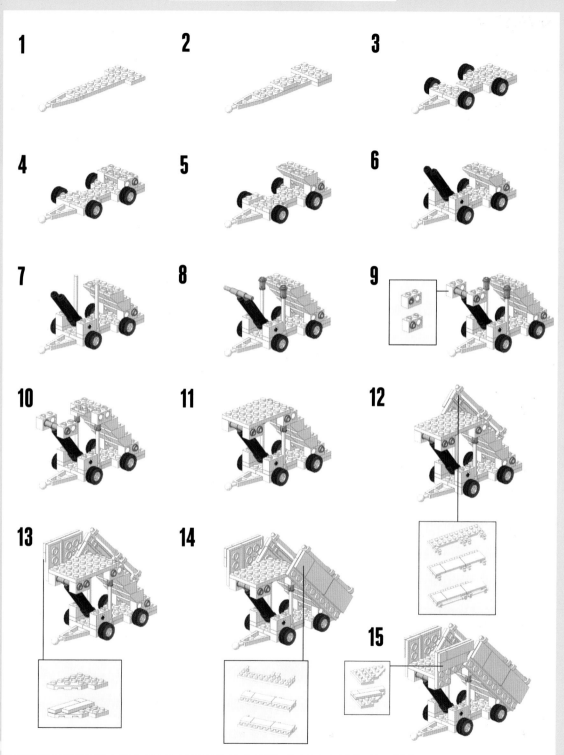

STEAM LOCOMOTIVE

The first full-scale locomotive was built by Richard Trevithick in 1804, and steam trains remained in common use for 150 years. These days most trains are electric or diesel, and travel on a steam train can be a rare occurrence. Even so, steam trains remain an iconic image worldwide.

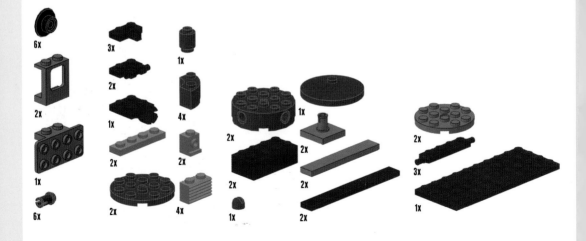

1

2

3

4

5

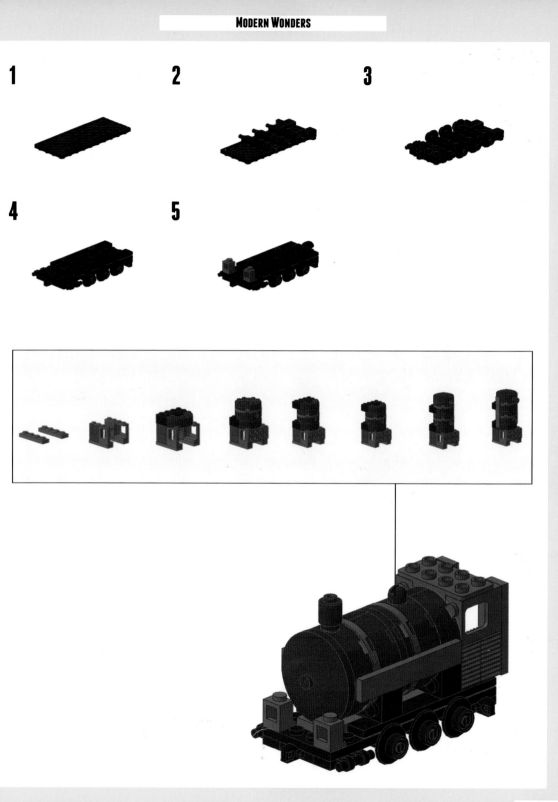

Ford Model T

It's often said that Henry Ford deemed his cars could be "any color as long as it's black," but actually the original Model T was available in many different colors and the cars have been painted into almost every color since. Our LEGO® model is based on a 1927 model which still exists—on display at The Henry Ford Museum in Detroit.

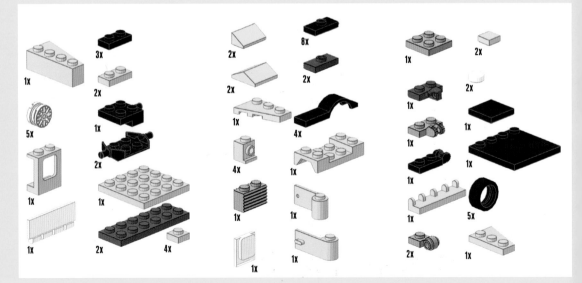

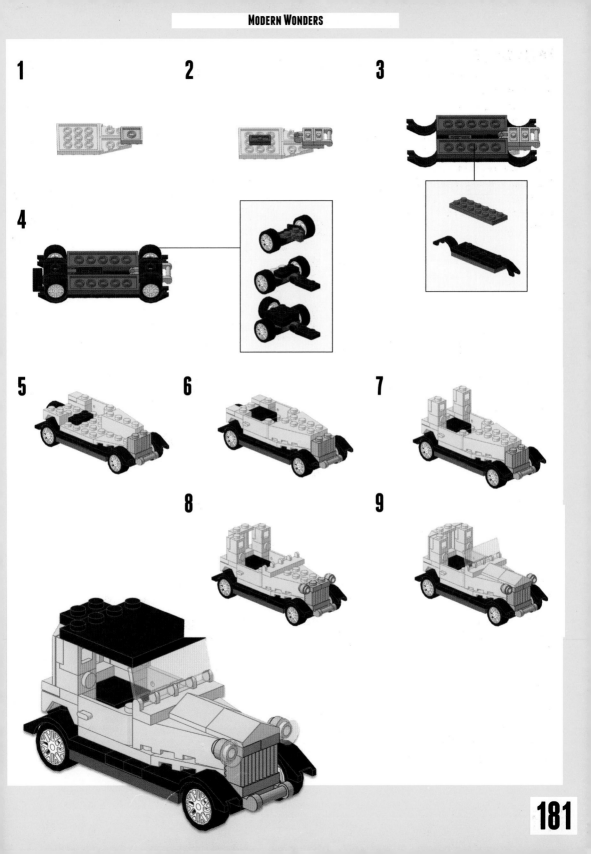

1

2

3

4

5

6

7

8

9

181

INTERNET

You might not stop to think just how it is that an email makes its way to your relatives in Australia, but it has to somehow. Encircling the world are thousands upon thousands of miles of submerged fiber-optic cables, carrying every email, "like," friend, streaming video, and of course telephone call. Our Silicon Valley cable map shows just how common these are. The colors represent the capacity of each cable from 250 (green) to 3,000 (red) gigabytes per second. How fast is that!

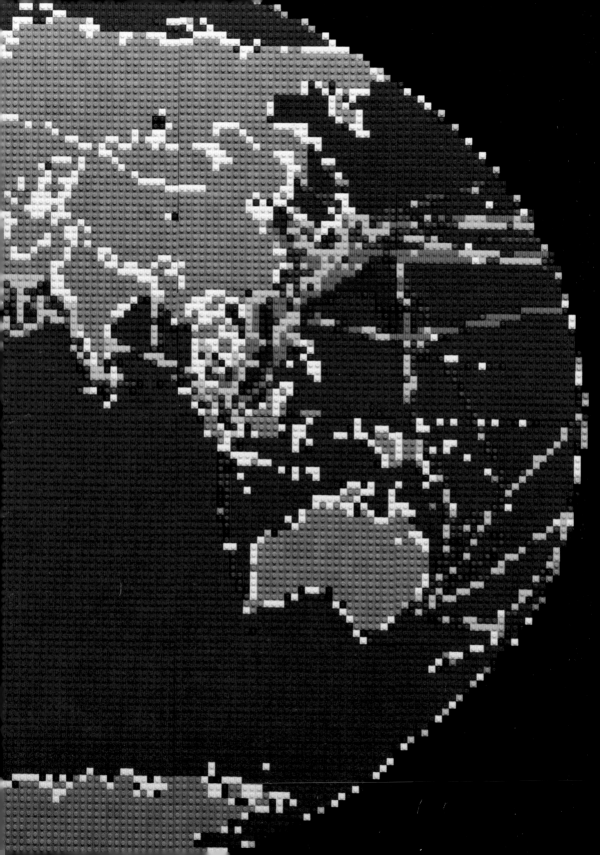

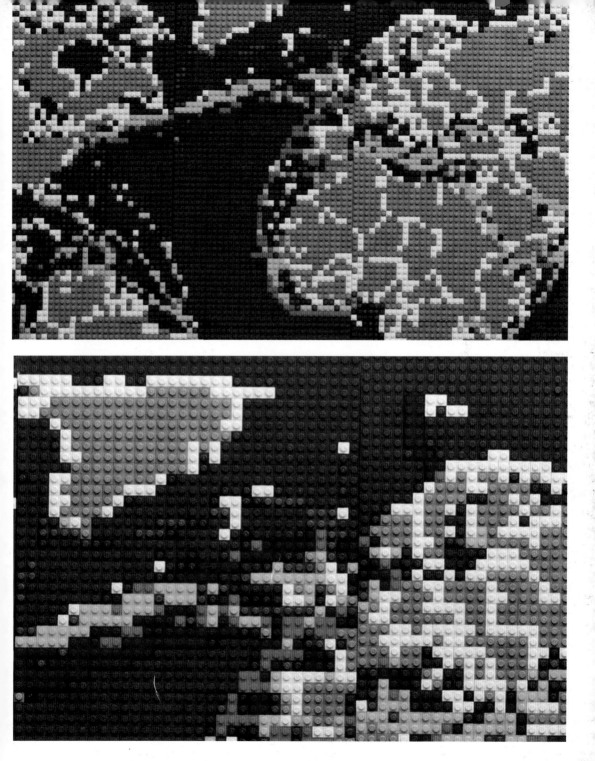

The fastest of these fiber-optic Internet cables could transfer a film from the United States to the United Kingdom, in full HD, in just ⅓₀₀th of a second.

TABLET COMPUTER

It's estimated that one third of Americans own a tablet computer, so this LEGO® tablet should hopefully look fairly familiar. We've used some custom printed tiles to represent the apps installed on our tablet, but you could use any decorated tiles you have in your collection.

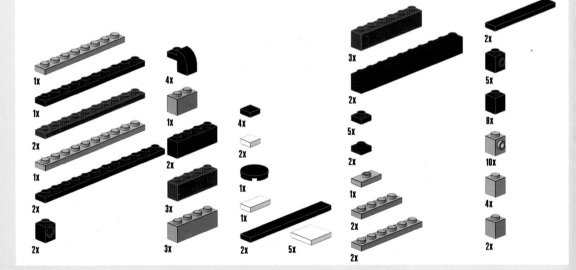

1x
1x
2x
1x
2x
2x

4x
1x
2x
3x
3x

4x
2x
1x
1x
2x

5x

3x
2x
5x
2x
1x
2x
1x
2x
2x

2x
5x
8x
10x
4x
2x

1

2

3

4

5

6

7

8

9

10

11

12

13

x2

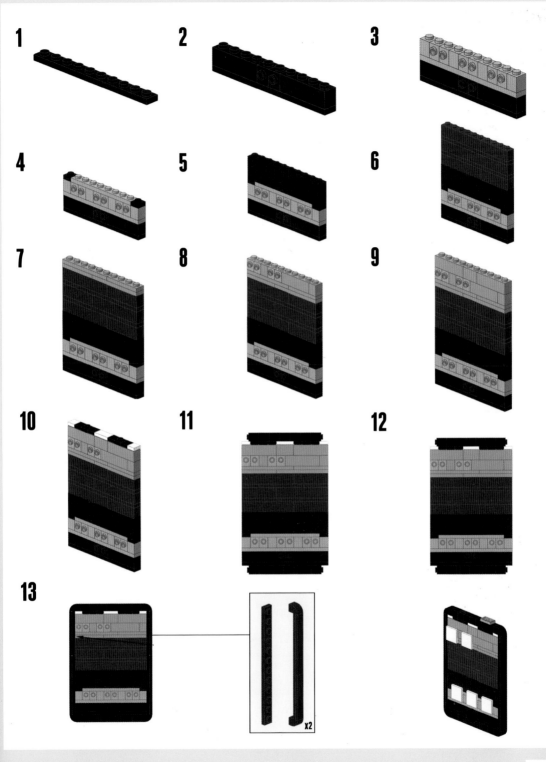

TWITTER BIRD

Although this social media logo might look like a simple shape, it was possibly the hardest model in the whole book to perfect. To achieve the smooth curves and angled feathers of this design, elements are placed not just upward but facing to the left, right, and downward. See *www.warrenelsmore.com/brickwonders* for additional detail.

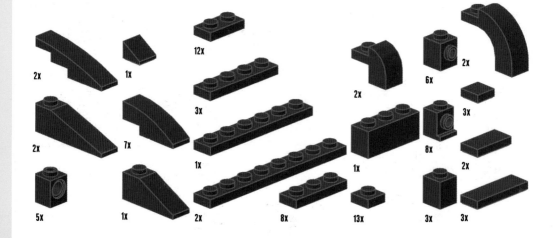

2x   1x   12x   2x   6x   2x

2x   7x   3x   2x   8x   3x

5x   1x   1x   1x   2x

2x   8x   13x   3x   3x

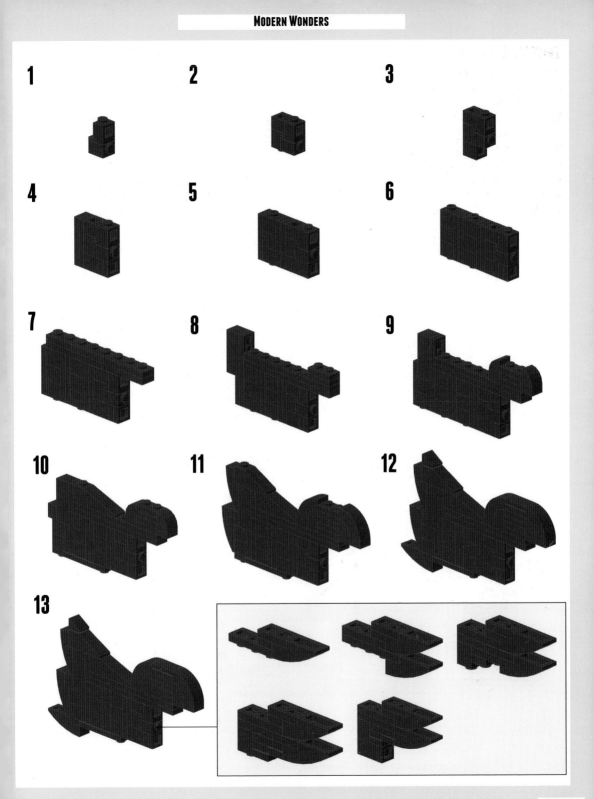

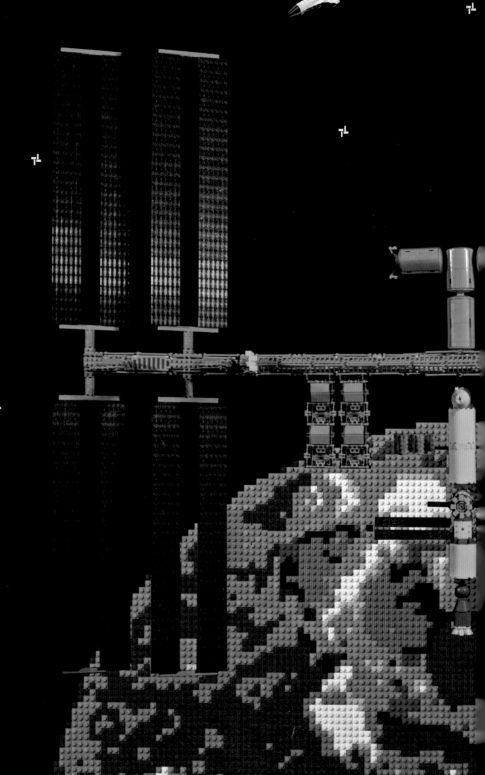

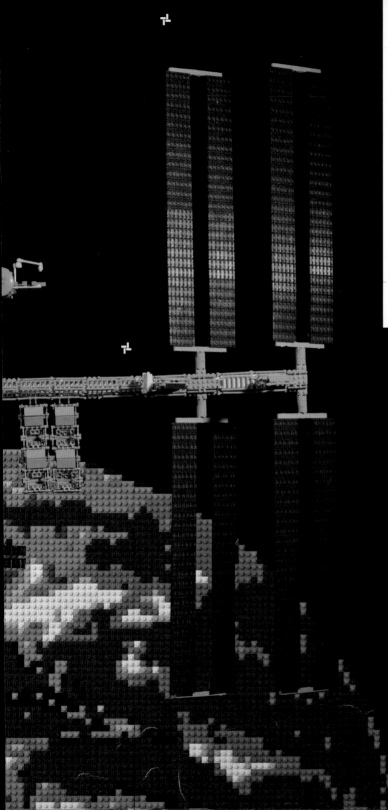

INTERNATIONAL SPACE STATION

The International Space Station (ISS) is the world's most permanent habitat in space, having been continuously occupied for more than 13 years. Built by the American, Russian, Japanese, European, and Canadian space agencies, it is a truly international effort. The station itself has taken more than 10 years to assemble and now measures over 230 feet (70 meters) long by 350 feet (107 meters) wide. That's a huge space, but only a fraction of this is pressurized to allow the crew to move around—about the volume of three school buses.

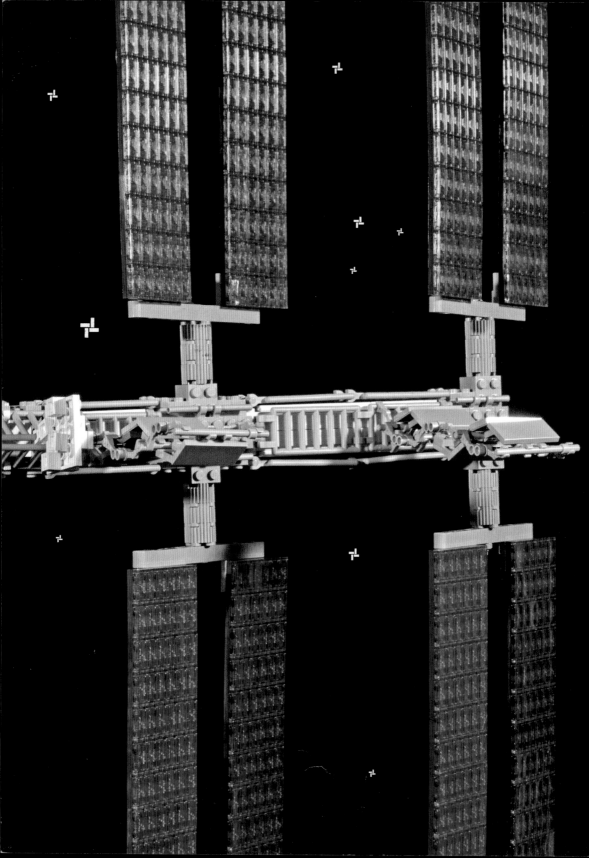

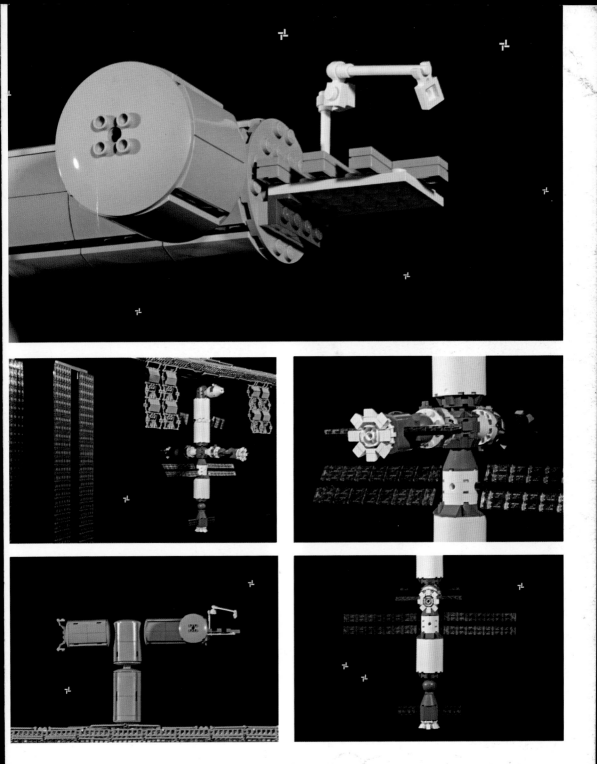

As the ISS is constantly evolving, our model shows how the station looked when this book was published, but it is sure to change over time.

SPACE SHUTTLE

NASA's Space Shuttle is perhaps the most iconic spacecraft ever built—transporting cargo such as the Hubble Space Telescope into space and then gliding back to Earth. Six shuttles were built, of which now only four remain because of the loss of Challenger and Columbia. The retired orbiters are now housed in museums across the United States.

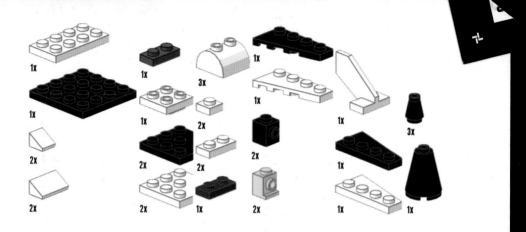

1

2

3

4

5

6

7

8

9

10

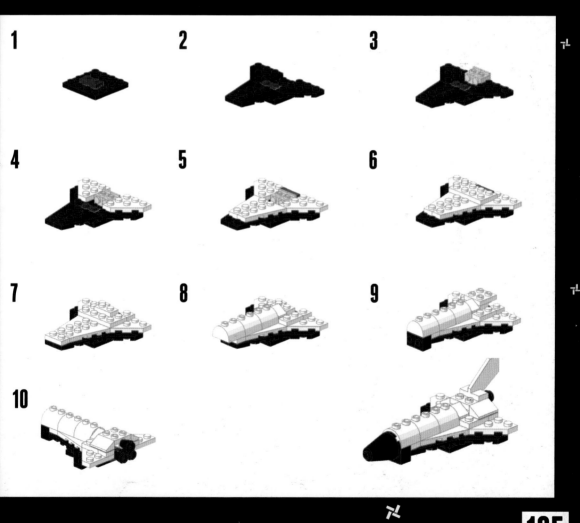

Soyuz Capsule

The *Soyuz* capsule is one of the oldest designs of spacecraft, first designed in the 1960s and still in use today. Of course, the capsule has been greatly updated since its launch, as it is now the only way of sending men and women to the ISS. It's also the astronauts' "life raft"—ready at all times for a quick escape.

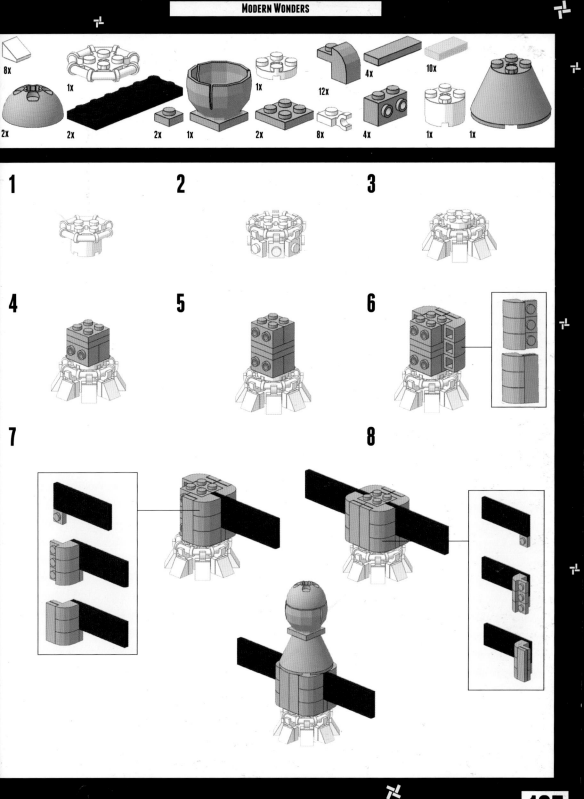

AURORA AUSTRALIS

Many people would have heard of the Aurora Borealis, a spectacular show of northern lights. Did you know, though, that there is a matching Aurora Australis over the South Pole? Both phenomena occur as charged high-energy particles hit the Earth's atmosphere, directed by our planet's magnetic field. In our model, we've created a LEGO® mosaic to try to show the majesty of these displays, which use more than 90,000 pieces alone.

Our intrepid explorers have left the British Halley VI research station to launch a weather balloon. It looks like they'll have to work through this cold snap!

WEATHER BALLOON

This LEGO® weather balloon is a great example of the "SNOT" technique from page 10. To make the rounded shape, LEGO plates are built in five different directions—not just up, but left, right, forward, and backward. The thinner plates enable a much smoother surface than would be possible with just bricks.

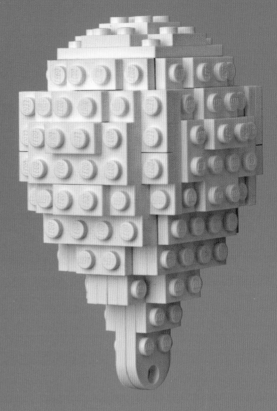

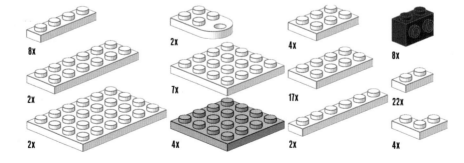

8x

2x

2x

2x

7x

4x

4x

17x

2x

8x

22x

4x

1

2

3

4

5

6

7

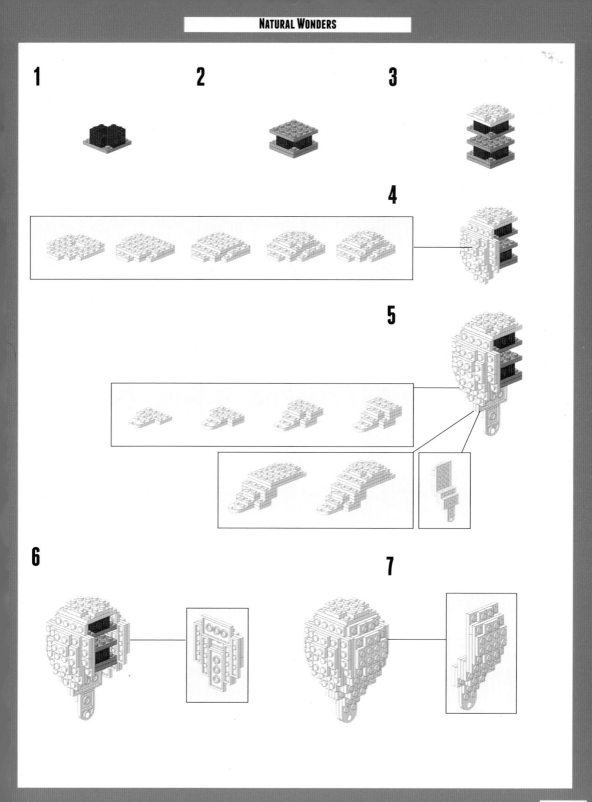

SNOWMOBILE

What better way to get around the Antarctic than on a snowmobile? These machines are perfectly suited to the frozen landscape. They use a pair of special skis at the front for direction and a track at the rear to provide traction on the snow.

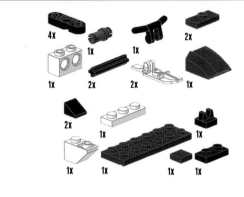

1

2

3

4

5

6

7

8

9

PENGUINS

Although penguins are associated with Antarctica, only a few species actually live that far south. These penguins won't have a problem with the cold though, built from just a few specially chosen LEGO® bricks. Like their real counterparts, these penguins have gathered in a large colony for warmth and protection.

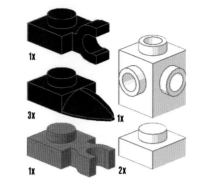

1x

3x   1x

1x   2x

1

2

3

4

5

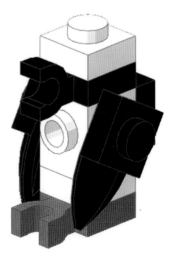

The Great Barrier Reef in Australia is unique. It is the largest coral reef in the world and covers an area of 133,000 square miles (344,400 square kilometers). That's the same size as the entire British Isles. What's more amazing is that the Great Barrier Reef is alive. It is made up of billions of individual coral polyps. These tiny animals live together in colonies to create what you might think of as a "coral."

Many coral polyps feed on sugars produced by algae which live within the coral structure of the Great Barrier Reef. Today this rare coral is under threat from the combined effects of pollution, overfishing, and global warming, and research into its protection is well underway.

CLOWN FISH

The clown fish lives among the tentacles of the poisonous sea anemone, but it doesn't get stung. The two animals live together—the clown fish protected by the stinging tentacles, and the anemone cleaned and similarly protected by the clown fish. It's a great example of symbiosis.

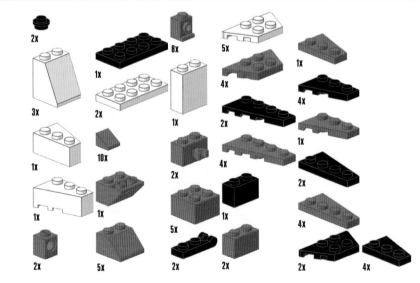

2x

3x

1x

1x

2x

1x

8x

10x

1x

5x

5x

2x

2x

5x

4x

2x

4x

1x

2x

1x

2x

2x

1x

4x

1x

1x

4x

2x

4x

2x

1

2

3

4

5

6

7

8

9

10

11

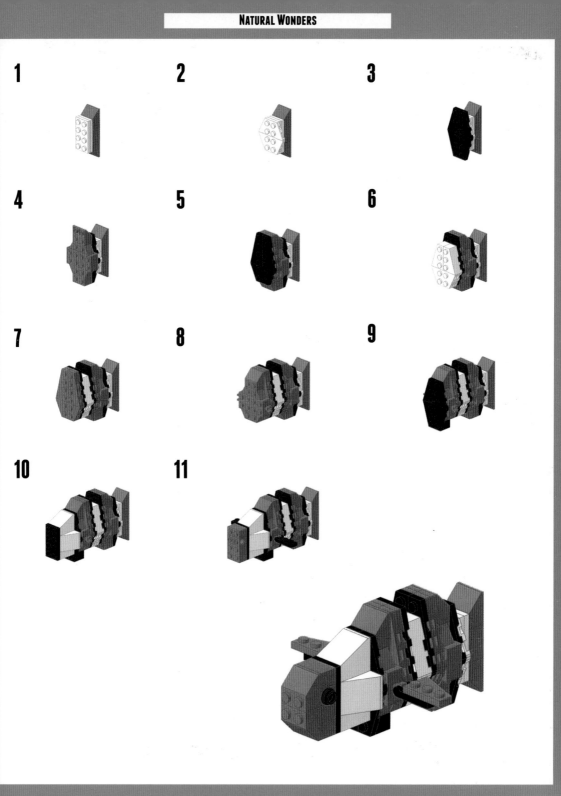

BUTTERFLY FISH

Butterfly fish are common in many areas of the Atlantic, Pacific, and Indian oceans. In fact, there are more than 120 specifies of these fish. In real life, they can vary in size from four to seven inches (11–18 centimeters) long, so our LEGO® model is not far from life-size.

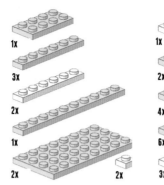
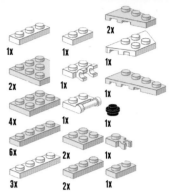

1

2

3

4

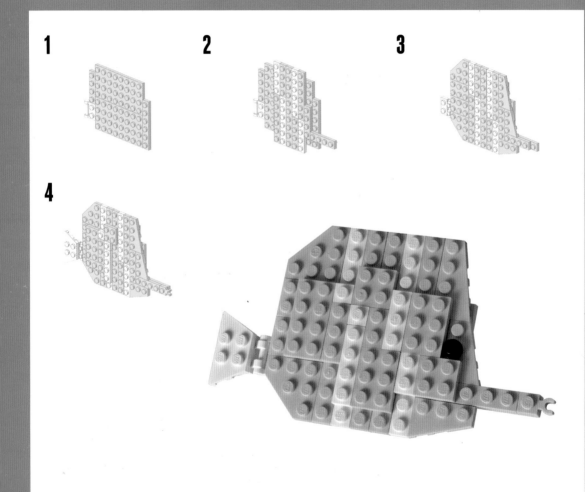

CORAL

Creating a coral reef from LEGO®
bricks isn't as hard as you might think.
Each of our types of coral is built
from a few pieces, repeated again
and again. This reflects the hundreds
and thousands of separate plants
and animals that make up a real life
coral reef.

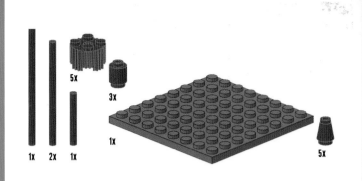

1x   2x   1x   5x

3x

1x

5x

1 **2** **3** **4**

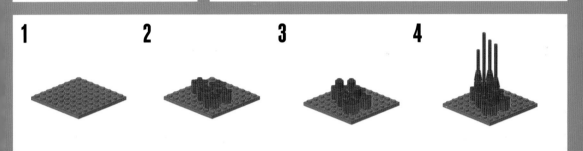

1

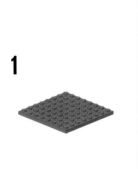

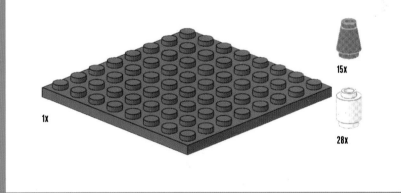

1x

15x

28x

2 **3** **4** **5**

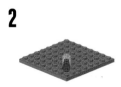

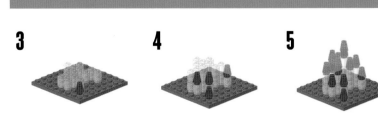

GRAND CANYON

The Grand Canyon's size is difficult to grasp unless you have visited it. Scoured from the earth by the Colorado River, it is almost 280 miles (451 kilometers) long, and in places 18 miles (29 kilometers) wide. Even more impressive is its depth. At certain places, the Canyon is over a mile (1,600 meters) deep. It has taken about 17 million years for the Canyon to form, as erosion from the river cut away into the rock.

The variety of weather in the canyon is astonishing. Temperatures can vary by 100 degrees Fahrenheit (38 degrees Celsius) from rim to base as a result of the drastic change in elevation.

HELICOPTER

A helicopter tour is a very popular way of seeing the Grand Canyon— especially from Las Vegas which is a four-hour drive away. These helicopters are built for luxury, though, enabling the passengers to get the best possible view of the canyon from the air.

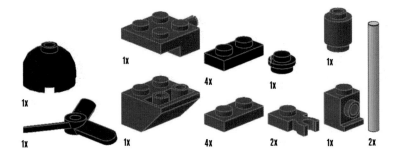

1x   1x   1x   4x   1x   1x

1x   1x   4x   2x   1x   2x

1

2

3

4

5

6

7

8

9

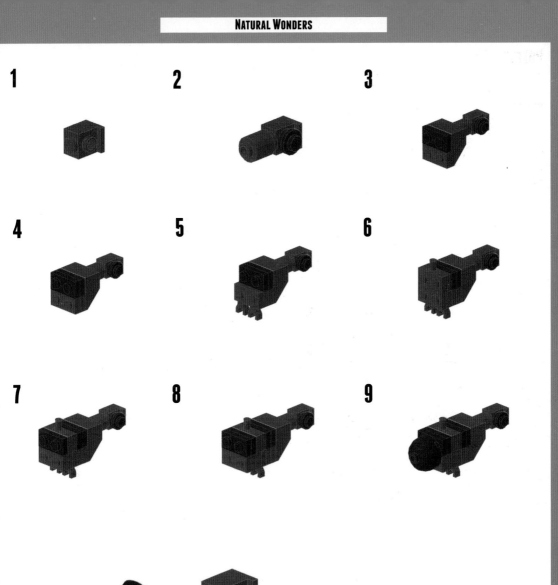

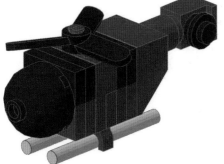

RAFT

A popular activity at the Grand Canyon is to go white water rafting along the Colorado River because you get a unique perspective from the water. Of course, it's also great fun too, though you are very likely to get wet as the rapids can be pretty fierce.

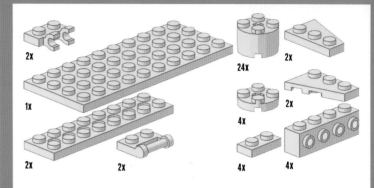

2x
1x
2x
2x
24x
4x
4x
2x
2x
4x

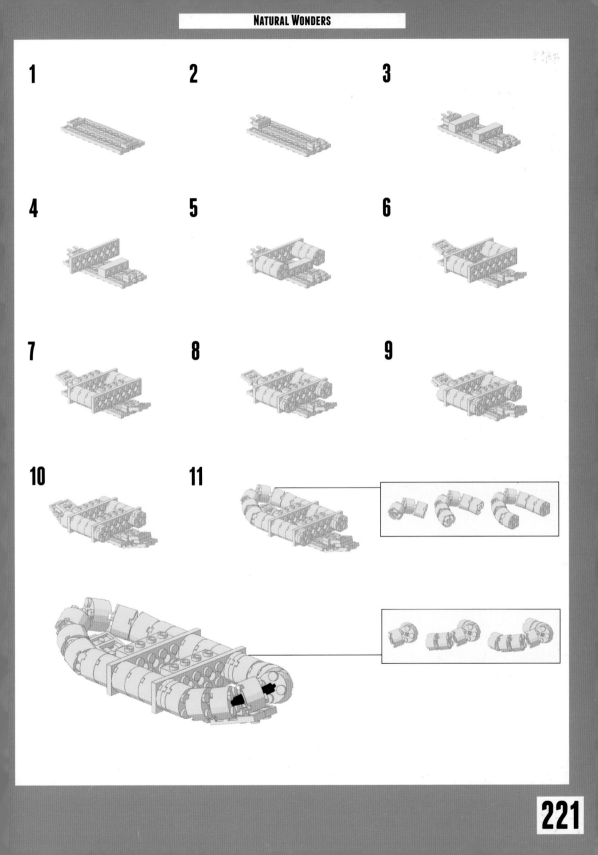

MATTERHORN

At 14,690 feet (4,478 meters), the Matterhorn is one of the highest peaks in the Alps, and its unique shape makes it emblematic of the whole region. The mountain has always attracted climbers, but it wasn't until 1865 that it was finally ascended—much later than many other peaks. Since then, however, the mountain has taken more than 500 lives, demonstrating just how difficult the ascent is.

The Matterhorn is situated in the Pennine Alps on the border between Italy and Switzerland. If you're just visiting the mountain as opposed to climbing it, you can take a cable car to a peak over 12,000 feet (3,700 meters) high. Don't worry, though, we won't tell anyone!

225

MINI MATTERHORN

This LEGO® model proves that sometimes you don't need any special pieces or complex building techniques to recreate something in LEGO bricks. This mini Matterhorn is built from only standard bricks, plates, and slopes. The distinctive shape of the mountain can easily be re-created—from this view, at least.

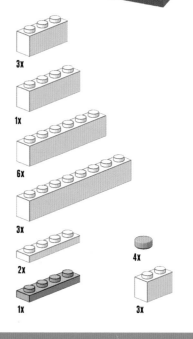

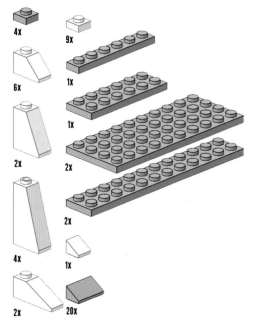

4x
9x
6x
1x
1x
1x
2x
2x
2x
4x
1x
2x
20x

3x
1x
6x
3x
2x
1x
4x
3x

1

2

3

4

5

6

7

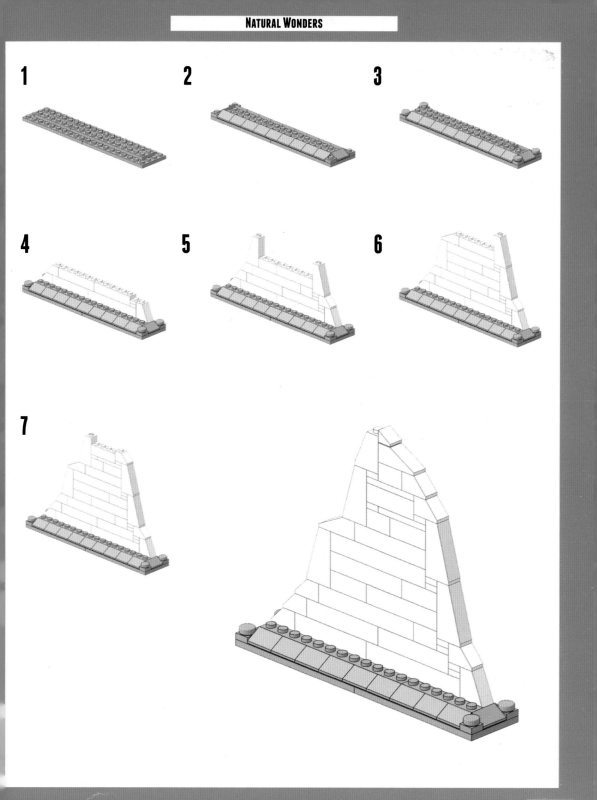

SWISS FLAG

Building a flag from LEGO® bricks isn't too complex—especially with a nice simple design such as the Swiss flag. This flag, however, flaps in the wind. By using round plates and square plates, it's possible to make the flag bend as if the wind has taken it. You can use this technique to make all sorts of curved surfaces from square LEGO bricks.

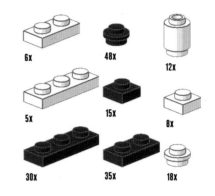

6x   48x   12x

5x   15x   8x

30x   35x   18x

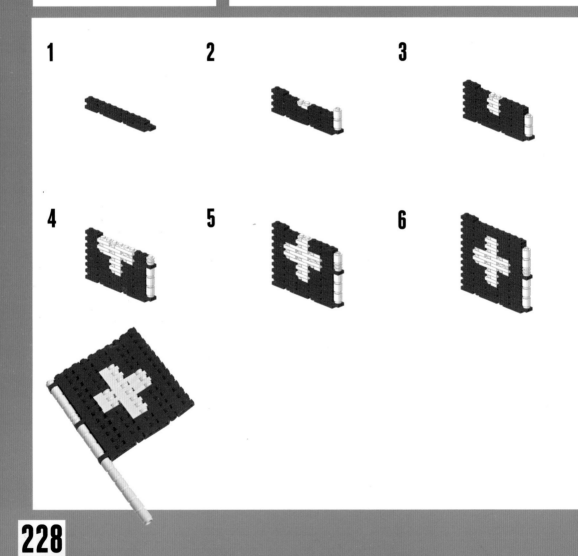

1

2

3

4

5

6

SWISS PENKNIFE

What could be more Swiss than a penknife? Don't worry about running with this one though, the blade isn't sharp enough to cause any real damage. And if you want to add more functions, it's easy to do with just a few more LEGO bricks.

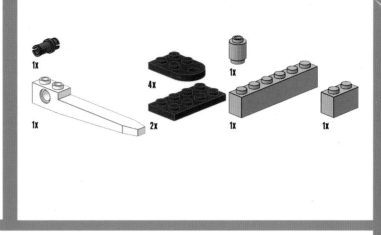

1

2

3

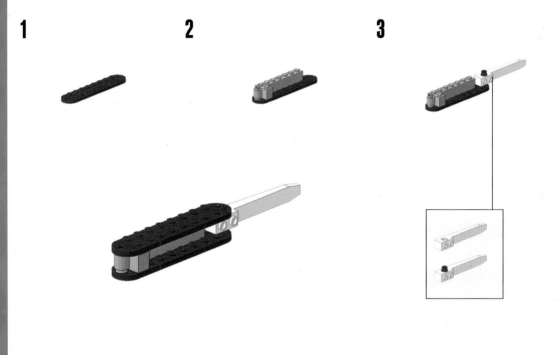

229

AFRICAN SAVANNA

Savannas cover around 20 percent of the world's land mass and are found on many continents. This scene represents the natural wonder that is the biodiversity of Africa. Though it's not too common to see elephants, giraffes, monkeys, ostriches, and crocodiles all together, at least it makes for a good photo opportunity.

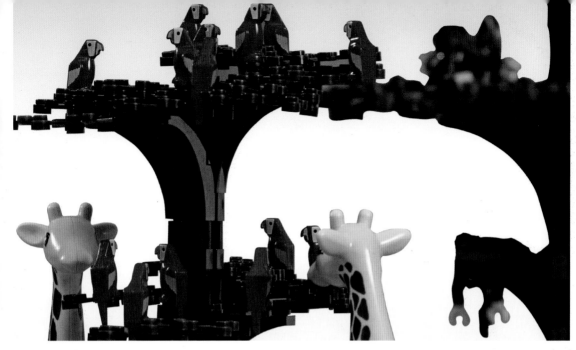

The animals we've used here are mainly LEGO® Duplo animals—good for younger children. Their bigger size fits perfectly with the LEGO tourists, and of course, they are too cute to ignore.

4x4 Vehicle

If you're on a trip to any wilderness, you'll need a strong, rugged vehicle to make sure you can get back again. This off-road 4x4 has big chunky tires to cross rough terrain, and a large seating area to carry the adventurers. Safety first, though—there's a spare tire on the hood just in case.

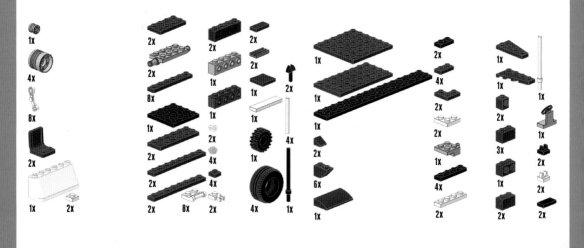

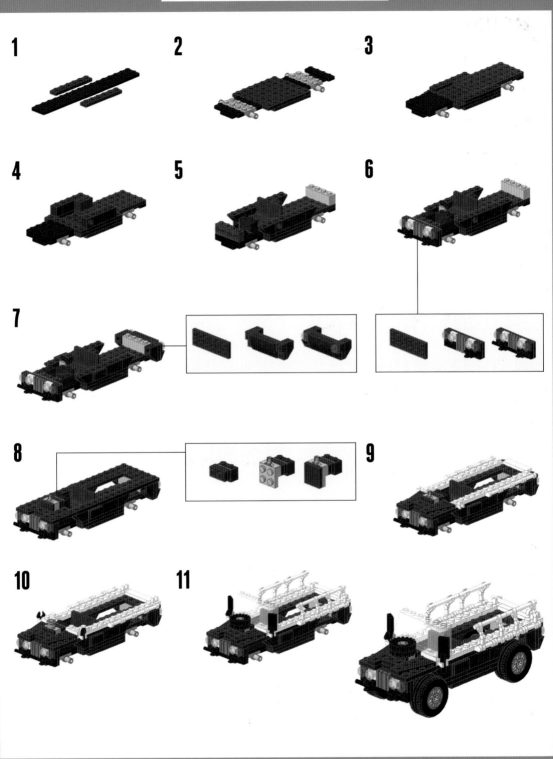

HOT AIR BALLOON BASKET

What better way to see the safari plains than from a hot air balloon? Real hot air balloons float because the hot air inside weighs less than that on the outside. Our LEGO® balloon weighs five and a half pounds (two and a half kilograms), though, so there's no danger of this one flying away with the passengers.

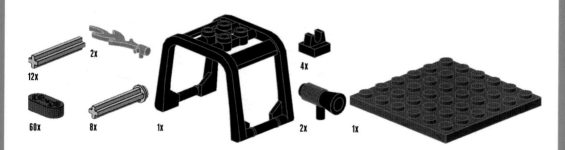

12x
2x
60x
8x
1x
4x
2x
1x

HA LONG BAY

Whereas you may not recognize the name, millions of people around the world will have seen the Ha Long Bay as a backdrop to films. It consists of nearly 2,000 individual limestone islands, many of which are hollow and contain huge caves. Each island is topped with thick jungle vegetation and is home to a number of unique species.

Ha Long Bay became a World Heritage Site in 1994, helping to protect its unique landscape. The area is the most popular tourist attraction in Vietnam and receives more than a million visitors every year.

VIETNAMESE BOAT

Long-tail boats are popular throughout much of South East Asia. Rather than a normal marine engine, they use standard car engines, mounted on long propeller shafts. This long shaft enables the motor to be placed well clear of the water, plus it also helps to keep the motor dry.

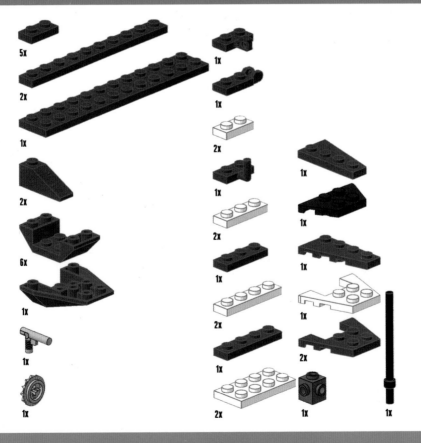

5x
2x
1x
2x
6x
1x
1x
1x

1x
1x
2x
1x
2x
1x
2x
1x
2x

1x
1x
1x
1x
2x
2x
1x
1x

1

2

3

4

5

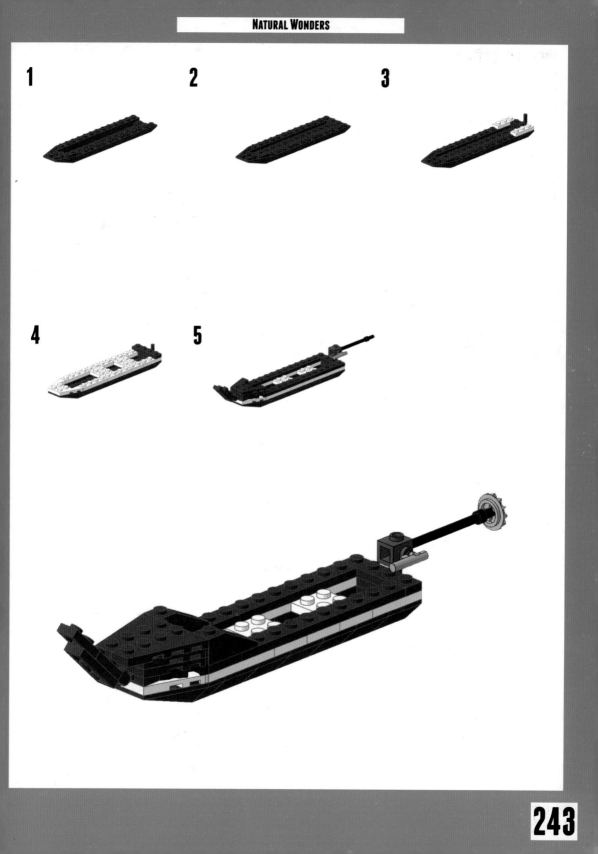

HA LONG BAY ISLAND

Why not build your own film set at home? This is one of the islands from the Ha Long Bay model. As all the islands are individual, it's easy to build them up slowly. Unless you want to re-create the whole bay, of course—then you'd need thousands of these.

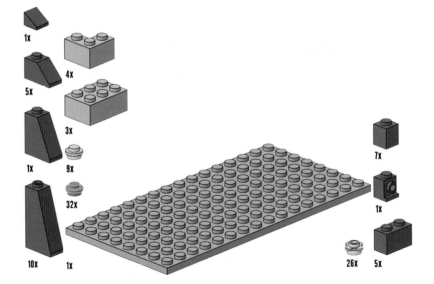

1x

5x

1x

10x   1x

4x

3x

9x

32x

7x

1x

26x   5x

1

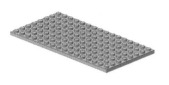

2

3

4

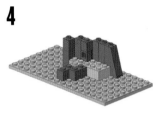

5

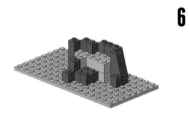

6

7

NIAGARA FALLS

The Niagara Falls are three waterfalls on the border between Canada and the United States, and are actually moving slowly backward as the underlying rock erodes. Each year, the three waterfalls move about one foot back toward Lake Erie from where the waterfalls are fed. The Bridal Veil, American, and Horseshoe Falls are separated by two small islands, and between them carry the highest flow of water over any waterfall in the world.

Dropping 165 feet (50 meters), the waterfalls carry four million cubic feet (113,000 cubic meters) of water every minute. That's enough to fill 45 Olympic swimming pools.

MAID OF THE MIST BOAT

The *Maid of the Mist* has been taking tourists to see the falls up close for over 70 years—or at least one of the boats has. The most recent addition to the fleet is the *Maid of the Mist VII*, which took sail in 1997. This is the model that our boat is based upon.

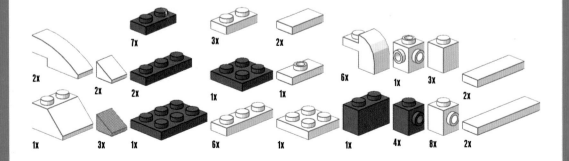

1

2

3

4

5

6

7

8

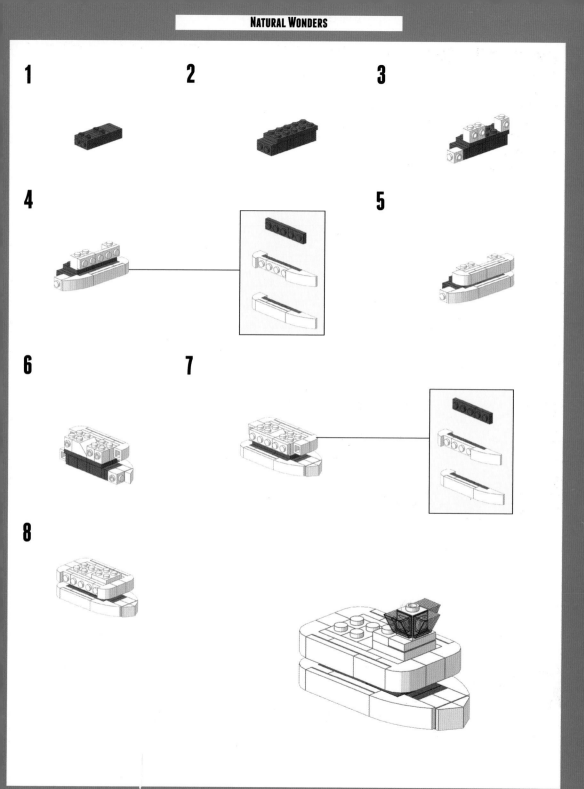

BARREL RIDE

Did you know that in the last 100 years, at least 23 people have gone over the falls? Although Annie Edson Taylor first used a barrel to go over the falls in 1901 on her 63rd birthday, the more modern attempts used specialized equipment. Don't try it, though—it's highly illegal in both the United States and Canada.

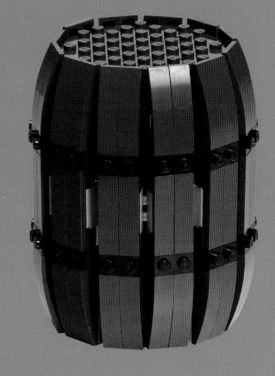

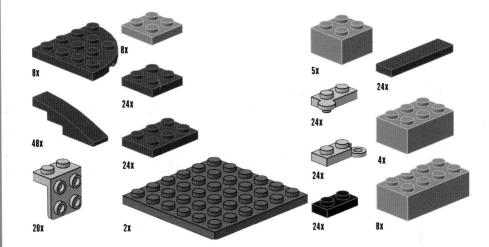

8x

8x

24x

48x

24x

20x

2x

5x

24x

24x

24x

24x

4x

8x

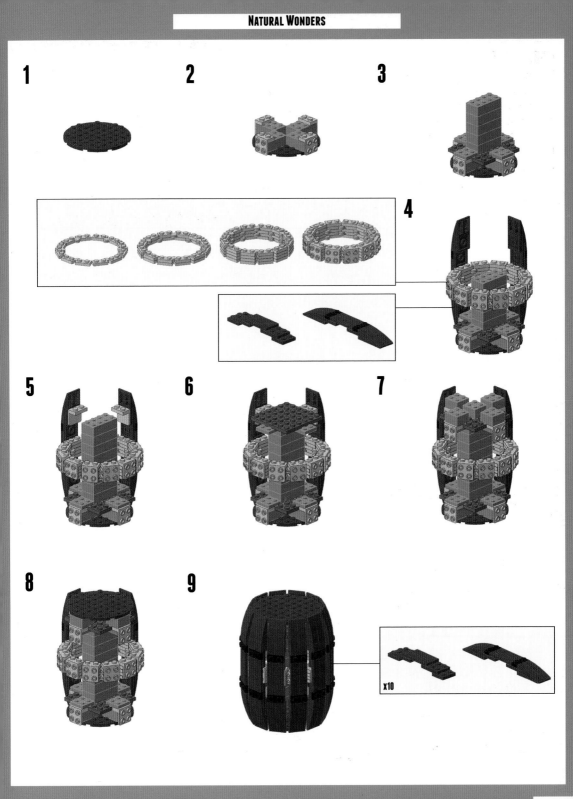

1

2

3

4

5

6

7

8

9

x10

INDEX

CREDITS AND RESOURCES

Kirsten Bedigan is a classical archeologist and ancient historian based in Edinburgh, UK. She was introduced to LEGO® as a young child and has not stopped playing with it since.

Teresa "Kitty" Elsmore was a LEGO fan as a child and continues to enjoy creating models with LEGO bricks today. Her passion is for organic forms, such as the trees and gardens you see in this book. One example of Teresa's work is the Great Barrier Reef on page 206, which vividly captures the colors and textures of the ocean. Since their marriage in 2005, Teresa and Warren have collaborated on a number of projects, and she is responsible for many of the minifig characters that bring models, such as the airport, to life. She has also been involved in many of the large projects of *Brick Wonders* by providing inspiration and placing tens of thousands of bricks.

Warren Elsmore is an artist in LEGO bricks and lifelong fan of LEGO, based in Edinburgh, UK. He has been in love with the little plastic bricks since the age of four and is now heavily involved in the LEGO fan community. Since rediscovering his love of LEGO at the age of 24, Warren has never looked back. After 15 years in a successful IT career, he moved to working full time with LEGO bricks in 2012 and now helps many companies to realize their own dreams in plastic.

Warren's first book, *Brick City*, was released worldwide to critical acclaim, and since then the models from the book have gone on tour in museums and galleries throughout the UK. As well as these, Warren also organizes a number of public LEGO events throughout the year. In 2014, he hopes to bring a LEGO show to the Edinburgh Fringe Festival in his hometown. You can see more about both Warren and his brick masterpieces at warrenelsmore.com.

Arthur Gugick is a high school math teacher based in Cleveland, Ohio. He was born and raised in New York City and has been a fan of LEGO for over 40 years. You can see more of his creations at gugick.com.

Simon Kennedy lives in Edinburgh, UK, and is studying theology. He has a life-long love of LEGO and a particular interest in modeling buildings and trains.

Steven Locke is from a family with many generations of deep-sea divers in Peterhead, Scotland, UK. He has been a fan of LEGO since the age of four and has not stopped building since. Steven's LEGO models are mostly influenced by outer space and sci-fi.

Nathan Sawaya is a New York-based artist who creates awe-inspiring works of art out of some of the most unlikely things. His recent global museum exhibitions feature large-scale LEGO sculptures. A full-time independent artist, Sawaya accepts commissioned requests and shows his art in galleries in New York, Miami, and Maui. Sawaya's art form takes shape primarily in 3D sculptures and oversized portraits. He continues to create daily while accepting commission work from around the world.

BUYING BRICKS ONLINE

If you don't have all of the parts required for some of the models featured in this book, or can't quite decide exactly which bricks I've used, then help is at hand. Complete lists of the parts you will need for each of the buildable projects featured in this book are available on my website, *warrenelsmore.com*.

If you need some but not all of the parts for a particular project, I recommend working from the full list and simply deleting the bricks (or the quantities of them) that you already have: this will allow you to buy only the parts that you need—not that having a few spares ever hurt anyone.